Stolen Sanity

Biodun Abudu

Biodun Abudu

www.BiodunAbudu.com

Copyright © 2019 by Biodun Abudu
All rights reserved
Printed in the United States of America

Art Work : Biodun Abudu
Graphics : Henry Jimenez

ISBN-10: 1733591001
ISBN-13: 978-1733591003

Previous Novel by Biodun Abudu: Tales of My Skin
Currently on Amazon.com

Biodun Abudu

STOLEN SANITY

IS

BASED ON A TRUE LIFE STORY

DISCLAIMER

Some names and identifying details have been changed to protect the privacy of individuals. I have tried to recreate events, locales, and conversations from my memories of them. In order to maintain their anonymity, in some instances I have changed the names of individuals and places. I may have changed some identifying characteristics and details such as physical properties, occupations, and places of residence.

DEDICATION
"To Those That Care"

I was walking the plank of my life and seeing death pass by, winking at me night after night. Looking glamorous on social media but bowing my head down as I walked by my fellow humans. I couldn't look into the eyes of the world, so I found a secret lonely place to hide, and I cried in the shower as the water covered my tears perfectly. There is no use trying to explain my sadness to anyone who hasn't stepped on bare glass, been beaten with iron rods, pierced with religion, and forced to swallow culture for the sake of a good family name.

I was always a mysterious boy who never understood why I cried even when I was holding onto happiness. I guess I still haven't found my freedom, I haven't found the right person to tell my story. I haven't experienced the moments I have dreamed about all my life: traveling to less popular places, climbing mountains naked, and looking at my body without seeing the scars that remind me of what I have been fighting half of my life.

While other children played with dolls, tennis balls, rubber ducks, and toy cars, I was somewhere crying under my bed, looking at the dark shadows coming closer and lashing me into years of buried sadness and unexplained depression. Home is not necessarily the place where my family dwells, but it's where I felt I didn't need to defend myself with every move and every word spoken from my lips. I've been at war with myself, battling flashes in my mind and uncontrollable emotions. I've been traveling with pain, bloody abominations, dark secrets, and sugar-coated insecurities, just seeking sanity in an endless journey to find my people.

- Biodun Abudu

PREFACE

In a trapped trance I was on a train ride to disaster. Riding with suicidal thoughts, hearing my rapist announce each stop in which he will commit sin upon my youthful temple. I suppose I could just let go of my mother's hands and exit to find my sanity and protection. However, with no guidance and no direction I will be left for another devil to prey upon me for his satisfaction.

In reality you can call me the queen of sorrow for I only know pain. Call me the princess of numbness for I have become a playfield for my uncle to test his manhood on constantly and I have become numb to the pain. I was the girl with the sealed padlocked lips for the sake of a good family name and to keep our fabulous Christian background pure until this very moment.

My five human senses suffered during my young days. I would be starved, dry in my mouth for days for trying to tell my mother about my rape. I would be told to close my eyes and I would receive his manhood forcefully and more brutally than the last time. My ears would suddenly become temporarily deaf after a pot was slammed into my ears by my mother for telling an outsider about my rape. My nose mostly recognized the smell of his sweat whenever he was on top of me or even the smell of my blood when he forced his way inside me. When I would touch, it would be to touch my thighs only to clean the blood dripping from my private parts when he forcefully let himself in.

With my summertime sadness, wintertime death wishes each day became worse. Born into a sinful world, I took my queue in line behind others. Born to suffer, I accepted my faith. Born to figure life out, I try and hit rock bottom to learn. Born to be defensive, I see everyone as my enemy. Born to die, I await my day to leave this cold world.

I knew my life would be an interesting journey from the very first tear I ever shed. I have never been able to stand on my own because I was told I was weak in my younger days. I've never seen the need to stand in front of a mirror because I've been told I'm ugly and not needed in this world. I accepted that message from my early childhood.

    Losing touch with reality because I have been trying to seek sanity within my family. Here I am dipping my hand in the pool of blood dripping from my private pool that my uncle has tampered with. There is no one to call, and even the pastor I look up to can't look beyond his heavenly high post to listen to me. He silences me in the name of Jesus before I can even say a single word. I may need prayer, but I don't need judgment - that's just another knife piercing my soul.

    I breathe, watching his hand crawl up and in between my thighs. He walked away with my heart, my sanity, my virginity, and my soul. He decided to forcefully let himself in with his whole world of wickedness and darkness. I ended up soaked with tears sitting in front of a therapist who had no idea what it felt like to wake up feeling like there might not be a tomorrow.

CHAPTER 1

Year after year, day after day, one must be thankful to the highest that our outer shells don't reveal all that we have been through on the inside. We must be thankful that the hurtful names people are quick to use like "bitch," "whore," "asshole," "cheater" or "old hag" aren't etched on our forehead after each and every horrible experience.

Have you ever wondered why people sometimes just give you a blank stare when you ask about their father or mother? It's usually because you are about to cross a dark and certain boundary. You have caught them off guard. They have gone through life strategically to avoid being in the presence of strangers who may ask such questions.

To be very careful, most will say "my mother is fine," or "my father is fine," but if you get comfortable enough to ask for details about them, then you may receive an outburst of emotions ending with: "I said, my mother is fine!!!"

Don't feel bad about the people who may react in such a manner, they have been programmed to act like robots to deny the pain, to shut the door on their emotions, and to paste a happy smile over any sorrow and regret.

It has been a very long time since I last looked back on where my life all started from and how my childhood began. Telling people my story is like flipping through actual pages of sadness.

I still can remember in those days living in little old Surulere, or to be more specific Aguda, which is located in Lagos, Nigeria. It feels like only yesterday and if I concentrate, I can still feel the intense heat from that burning sun. Aguda was an area in Surulere which was made up of rich, middle, and lower-class people all living together.

The middle-class people all stayed together in a deep corner at the very end of Surulere, and they kept to a common routine. They would dress very normal, and drive mid-range cars until it was time for parties, and then they would go 'all out' with their expensive clothing and cars. The women were primarily traders who sold African laces and owned fashion boutiques.

The upper class be dressed all-out all the time, no matter what, as they wanted to remind you of their status on a daily basis. The rich people often suffered a stigma that their hard-earned money was from a spiritual ritual which involved killing someone or doing spiritual or blood sacrifices for money.

The lower class mainly worked as teachers at the primary schools, and the extremely lower class handled the minutia of daily life, like transportation and food. The men were conductors hanging on the doors of public buses, while the women roamed the streets selling products carried on their heads, often with their children trailing along behind them.

Many of these women were corner road cooks who would sit in front of an enormous frying pot full of hot oil and prepare native dishes like puff puff (made from a wet mix of flour, yeast, sugar, and water), and dun dun (fried yam) and plantain to be eaten with a very spicy red pepper stew.

If you thought a lady with such a business might have to have a register to hold the money she received from her salivating and hungry customers, then think again. These ladies usually stored their money wrapped in their skirts or head ties. They showed no shame untying their head wraps or slightly unwrapping their skirts to get change.

Even though these women were lower class, you could never ever make the mistake of paying them with Nigerian coins. They would rain down curses or throw the coins back, because nobody really dealt with coins, even the mallams, which are equivalent to corner stores in the U.S..

The mallams (sometimes called aboki stores) were about the size of bathroom stalls - there was one person inside, and the customers would look in from the outside, pointing to the product they wanted to purchase. My mind often wondered if there could also be a lady hiding under there, giving the clerk a blow job, but that was highly unlikely, because most women don't give blow jobs in Nigeria.

If a woman was present in the mallam's little store, she was probably just lying there waiting for him to attend to his customer and then get back to promising her the world and plenty of money. But in the end, all she would get would be tons of kids and a husband with a bad attitude trying to avoid his reality. Every time I hear the word mallam I think of the mallam's wife on our street who killed her neighbor's dog. It struck me as funny.

She was always getting caught bending down and pulling back her skirt to pee in the gutters. The owner of the shop had warned her multiple times to stop, and even threatened to hire thugs to beat her up if she was caught peeing there again, but the mallam's wife was very stubborn. One evening, the entire street was filled with horrendous screams, and we ran out to find the mallam's wife crying and rolling on the floor in pain. We later found out that the owner of the shop had sent her dog to deal with the mallam's wife, and the dog had taken a deep bite out of her butt cheek as soon as she stooped to pee. A few weeks later the mallam's wife sought out revenge by pouring acid on the dog. The dog died a few hours later from the acid burn.

All three of the classes had one thing in common, they all made sure to return to their homes by an early enough hour to avoid being visited by armed robbers, or harassed by the night watch guards who would stop them to make sure they lived in the street before the gates would open. Even innocent college kids could end up getting shot if they came home drunk and made the mistake of arguing with the night watchmen who had mistaken them for armed robbers.

In Aguda the streets were narrow and rough and filled with potholes, dusty corners and muddy lanes. There were no traffic lights, so cars went wherever they wanted, causing accidents and running over children and the elderly. The street gutters were filled with trash, and when it rained the trash would flow through the water and land in people's compounds. The gutter water was filled with tadpoles and strange black remnants, and I hated walking when the rains flooded the streets, knowing all sorts of things could be living in the water.

In those days, I would wake up smiling in the mornings for many reasons. For one, I was happy to see the real world once again and escape from the nightmares of being chased that haunted me whenever I slept. They got so bad that I often woke up to a bed soaked with urine or a pillow drenched from tears and sweat.

For another, many people I knew had gone to bed and never woken up again, and I didn't want to be one of the growing number who were dying in their sleep. Waking up from such a nightmare reassured me that I had survived and was still truly alive.

On Sunday mornings I woke up really early so that I could shower before any of the others in the house woke up. I made sure that if I spilled water I also mopped it up, because it was one of the little things that could set my mother off. I looked forward to Sundays the most, because it meant I would get to show off my new Sunday dress. It was the only day my clothing wouldn't raise questions about my mother's financial responsibility, because she made sure I always looked my best in the presence of people from church.

    I would spend hours in front of the mirror in the room I shared with my older sister. I spent so much time adding glitter to my cheeks, adjusting my ponytail, and putting in my hair ribbons. My side of the bedroom was like a doll house, with everything included, even a picture of my huge crush that I hid behind my baby powder.

    I thought I was the prettiest in my family, but I dared not say that out loud or my sisters would beat me up. It was evident though in the time I took to make sure I was noticed and looked my feminine best. Even at a young age I made sure everything was on point, from my sticker play color nails, to my hair, shoes, dress, and more.

My mum usually fed us yam and eggs every Sunday morning, and I always kept myself on guard from soiling my dress even without her telling me. Whenever I soiled my dress she made it very clear that she hadn't wanted to buy me the dress in the first place because of how careless I was when eating, but I still smiled anyway, despite her criticisms.

Sundays were church days and there were churches on literally every street corner. You could hear praise and worship songs blaring from the loud speakers used to attract people traveling along the roads. My church was called The Reach Christian Church of God. Over the years, The Reach Christian Church of God started to become more of a fashion show than a place of worship. The members started arriving late intentionally, so that they could walk in while the pastor was preaching, and the women would have the perfect opportunity to show off the long trains on their dresses, and the men their sunglasses and nice suits. As time went on, the clothes on the women got more tightly fitted, slight cleavage started to show, and the skirts got shorter.

I felt like whatever my parents reported to the pastor, the next Sunday he would claim he had a vision, and share my parent's words as though they came from the Lord. Churches in general, not just Nigerian churches, were losing sight of promoting love.

All they focused on was the sins of mankind. If you smoked - you're going to Hell, listened to pop music - you're going to Hell, drink alcohol - you're going to Hell, and the list went on and on. The pastors wouldn't help you overcome an addiction by referring you to a treatment center though, instead they would most likely label your sin from head to toe before they would even start to pray with you.

I always believed in taking action in addition to praying. I don't believe in simply praying alcoholism out of a person, but in taking action like grabbing the bottle away and taking him to recovery classes first, and then praying once those steps are already in place. When I would tell my pastor about something that happened at home, I expected him to have a conversation with my mother, pray, and keep track of the situation. However, most times, rather than hearing me out, he would just remind me of the little things I may have done in the past which my mother had told him about, instead of listening to me.

One time, when I was only five years old, I mentioned that my mother had thrown her heel at me. He instructed me, a little five-year old girl, to respect my mother, kneel, and apologize to her, despite the fact that the heel she threw at me had given me a black eye. He told me it was normal in our culture for a mother to lift whatever was close to her to strike a child for being stubborn.

He said he would pray the stubbornness out of me. "Stubborn acts and behavior are bad, and are of the devil," he would repeat over and over. But isn't it even more devilish to look at an innocent child who is still learning right from wrong and easily throw a shoe at her face for punishment? My mother treated me with abuse, and the pastor treated me with neglect -

these were the lessons I swallowed into my soul.

There were times I would avoid the pastor and talk to his wife instead, thinking she would be more concerned about the abuse I was receiving. I told her I was dragged out of bed by my hair one day because I overslept and missed the school bus. She responded, "Why didn't you wake up on time when your sisters were waking up? I'm sure you just went back to sleep. Now go and apologize to your mother for wasting time and gas that day when the school bus could have taken you."

In my impressionable state of mind, the words of the pastor's wife let me know that it would also be okay to pull my future daughter's hair for waking up late. There were no establishments that dealt with child abuse, your parents owned you, they were free to come up with whatever new and improved punishments they wished. The phrase, "Spare the rod and spoil the child," took on a darker tone over the years as little spanks from the hand progressed to horse whips, cable wires, and even frying pans if possible. If that was the culture we accepted, who would dare challenge it? Instead you bowed down in position, and humbly received the scars and marks upon your body.

Every Sunday, after we had heard the words of the Lord, most families would hang around for a yoghurt drink called Fango and a red-colored drink called zobo. I personally was on a mission, and would intentionally wait just a little bit longer, in order to get a glimpse of my crush, - the pastor's son. His name was Mayowa Adigun and he was like an angel that God had created, not made, but crafted specially for me. He was so perfect, and his smile was simply breathtaking. I had never spoken to Mayowa, but I was very sure back then that we would grow up and marry each other.

I had even sketched the perfect wedding dress in the diary that I had hidden under my bed. It would be covered with lace, diamonds, and pearls, and make such an unforgettable impact that people would be talking about it all over the world. I even fantasized that after the wedding I would be approached by an international museum asking to put my dress on display. Gosh, I was such a dreamer back then, but before I get carried away with my fantasy let me properly introduce my fabulous self.

    My name is Funke Adedayo, and I have two older sisters: Funmi Adedayo and Sandra Olatunji. Funmi and I had the same father who was a police officer, and our elder sister Sandra has a different father entirely, who was an engineer. I'm not too sure what happened between our father and my mother, or Sandra's father and my mother.

    Sandra always tried so hard to see her father. She sought his approval for almost everything she did. When she brought home good grades from school she would show her dad first before our mother. But Sandra's dad had moved on with his life and had another woman who had given him more kids, and even a son. - Sandra couldn't begin to compete with that.

Once in a while Sandra would tell us that she hated us and cause general havoc in the house in the hopes that my mother would send her off to her dad's place. Once my mother figured out this habit of hers, Sandra would instead be locked in her room or cut off from her father for a long while to discipline her.

CHAPTER 2

Confessions of a suicidal virgin

Dear Uncle,

I was at school thinking of you and how you caused me to live with the regret of being born into this cold world. I've been broken since the first time you shattered my virgin walls, it's okay though, I haven't told my mum yet, and I probably won't since she doesn't care anyway. Till this day I have not been able to figure out why you chose to destroy me with horrible memories and regrets. You took advantage of my innocence, my precious lips and my sacred temple. Disregarding my age, you boldly committed this abomination upon your own little niece.

Sorry I'm writing this letter, especially since you have found ways to avoid me. I may be broken, but I am hoping that this letter will reach you safely. I am writing this letter because I want you to know the pain I felt throughout my youth, so that when I do kill

*you, you can understand why I did it as you look back from the pit of Hell where you belong. Even the devil wouldn't recognize you. I will put a stop to this immorality and I am praying and hoping you are not out there doing the same to other little girls. I may pull the trigger on myself right after I finish you off. I think I will cut off your manhood and place it in your hands, since it was in your hands right before you broke my virgin walls, but for now may your soul rest in peace.
Thank you,*

Suicidal Virgin

There comes a time in one's life where there will be a continual flow of tears. The rain seems to take over day after day. No one is normally present to share your pain, not even present to listen. I wish someone could have told me that days like this would come. In the world we live in, it is so easy for people to sit on their couch and say the decisions that I made were stupid. You scream for help and when someone finally comes around to help you off the floor, you smile. But that smile suddenly turns to sadness when the man who pulled you up from the floor begins to unzip his pants.

    For some women, the first man to break their heart was their dad. That heartbreak is so painful it becomes almost impossible to trust love when it presents itself again. Every day is a reminder of what is missing from your family portrait, as family has become the definition of pain. The school days are a constant reminder of what you don't have, watching all your classmates with their fathers and mothers hugging them before they even strap on their seat belts.

At the front door of our house, I always took a moment to gasp for air before I could twist the knob. I never knew what to expect from my mother who was supposed to protect me. My mind was already damaged from being called a bastard and told I'm the devil. Abuse had made a home in our family, and insecurities stared back at me from the mirror since there was no one to tell me anything differently. Pain was swimming in my blood, it marinated into my system and controlled my happiness.

I have come to believe that every tear has a deeper story. It may be from a rape that is hidden within the family. It could be from a forced marriage at the age of 11 under the umbrella of culture. Sometimes it's from the daily physical blessing our husbands give us during vicious arguments. If my tears could talk, they would unleash the secrets I hide behind my smile. My makeup transforms me into a whole new person, it hides my flaws and the scars that remind me of my attempts at suicide. My dress also has a lot to say though the rips and blood stains, or even that I wore it in the first place to simply impress the devil I settled for along the way.

CHAPTER 3

In our early family portraits I would be the one in the front, smiling extremely hard and sitting in the middle with so much confidence. Believing in the perfect life, looking at my sisters and my mum, and thinking to myself that I felt blessed to have them. What was pain to me at such a young age? It was nothing because everything was perfect . . . well that's what most people believed. Most of our family portraits were just myself, my mum, and my two sisters - our fathers were rarely present. We hardly ever smiled in the later portraits, except when I forced myself too after a hard knock on my head from my mother. Many would say that in our family I was the most cheerful, and the easiest to talk to.

My mum was a police officer with a high position at her station. She made it clear wherever she went that she was the boss. I remember when she would come to my school to drop me off in her uni form. As she parked the car for me and Funmi to get out, she would also get out to have a talk with my teacher. She always made sure they did their jobs and did not cross their boundaries as far as disciplining me or seizing my school items.

Sometimes the conversations didn't end well, and she would call her officers to come and handcuff the teacher in the presence of my fellow students. For the rest of the school day I would be labeled "the police officer's daughter," and thanks to my mum there would be no more lectures for that particular subject that day because our teacher had been taken to the police station.

It started to cause bad feelings with classmates, not to mention their parents. I vividly remember one day when my mother came to pick me up and wasn't in uniform; one of my classmate's mums walked over to her and planted a huge slap on her face over something I can't even remember. The next thing I knew, my mum was reaching for her baton and whacked it all over the lady's body from head to toe.

The lady was in serious pain and was carried away to the police station. I don't know what happened next, only the hatred I felt afterwards from my classmate who cried over his mum. There were rumors among the students that after the police officers had beaten her, my mother poured bleach all over her bruises and had the police officers tie her down in the hot sun.

Even in our compound, my mum was boss - the tenants feared her, and they dared not show disrespect to my grandmother or they would face her wrath. The tenant's children were friends of mine and went to the same primary school. Practically everything that happened at home in our compound became a topic of discussion the next day at school. It became an important gist - gist is what we called juicy gossip in Nigeria.

I noticed the way people began acting differently towards me, and I knew they had been gossiping behind my back because whenever I had a quarrel with someone, suddenly they would drop a bomb about something they had heard about happening at my compound as a way to embarrass me. While many in the outside world feared my mum, it was a different story within my family. My aunts and uncles all challenged my mum and it often became physical, but she couldn't arrest any of them for fear of disrespecting my grandmother. I have a very minimal memory of my grandmother, but I do know she was tough! She mostly sat outside her door guarding our compound and sending away any visitors that didn't dress right or looked like criminals.

    I witnessed this firsthand one day when she sent away a new tenant's daughter, that she had never met, calling the girl a prostitute simply because she had on a short skirt. In my grandmother's mind she was right, and she reported it to the girl's mother, not knowing that she already knew and was very mad at my grandmother for embarrassing her daughter. The girl's family moved out the following month.

    Next to the worn-out iron chair in which my grandmother spent her days was her old yellow Volvo.

The only times she used it was when she hired a driver for a day to take her to one of her buildings where a tenant was past due on rent.

She owned many houses and businesses and she kept all of the money she collected in huge bags stored inside her house, so we dared not be caught walking in there without her knowledge. My grandmother didn't believe in keeping her money in a bank, she had a personal vendetta against them.

I remember once my cousin asking me if I ever wondered why one of my aunts would randomly come by early in the morning to fetch water for our grandmother. My cousin told me that my aunt would bring the water in from the well in a huge bucket, but when she would come out of the house, that same bucket was filled with money, which she would dump into her car boot. My aunt repeated this routine until our grandmother's big black drum was filled with water, so if it took 10 buckets to fill up the big black drum, then she left the house with that same amount of buckets filled with naira notes.

My grandmother was suspicious of us all. Even when she sent one of us into her house to get her something, she would start screaming after 2 minutes thinking we were going through her belongings. She was the type of woman who woke up early in the morning to pray to the Lord and then the very next minute was swearing and cursing at her tenants, saying: "a car will hit you for not bringing my money today" or "your children will die unexpectedly."

My grandmother fought constantly with her tenants and would even stand up on her bad leg to rip their shirts and slap their faces. Like many elderly people, she used a chewing stick in place of a toothbrush, and if she was in too much pain to stand up that day, we had to be extra careful or she would throw her green cup of saliva at us. My mum may not have been one of my Grandmother's favorite daughters, but it was very useful to have a police officer on call when her tenants proved to be stubborn about paying their rent.

My grandmother was the master of hoarding, she never wanted to throw anything away. She could keep a plate of eba (cassava) sitting for three days and would still eat it with fresh soup, and she would rain curses on you if you dared to throw it in the garbage.

Her home was like a family reunion for the rats that wandered in during the night looking for food. They would start out hiding under her car, and eventually find their way into her home. One time I heard some loud noises coming from under the couch she was sitting on and I tried to tell her it was a shrew, but she threw me out thinking I was just trying to get the money she had in her pouch by the chair. That shrew made a playground of her feet as it ran back and forth, but she felt nothing at all.

Along the way my sisters Funmi and Sandra grew wings, and it wasn't to fly towards positive things in life but rather to face off with the head boss-my mum. It seemed like the older we grew the more they developed the courage to challenge her during arguments.

From the outside they may have been viewed as disrespectful, but the truth is my mum never really helped the situation either. We already didn't have a close connection to our fathers and now the connection to our mother was starting to fall apart as well. A big part of it was that when our mum wanted to punish us, she would treat us exactly like the people she arrested every day. We could never just have a sit-down talk, in fact it was considered disrespectful to have a conversation with her about the kinds of personal things that girls want to ask their mum about.

    Historically, family love is believed to be one of the strongest bonds there is, the TV shows we watched even had regular family dinners, but I never experienced anything like that. In my home, we wouldn't even dare eat in the same room as my mum, if we tried she wouldn't utter a word, just gave us a look that said "get out." We ate in the hallway or in our rooms, and the maids ate right in the kitchen and they had to eat quickly and finish before my mum did. The dinner gathering should have been a way to keep the whole family updated on each other's lives, but I must confess that I didn't know much about my own sisters even though they lived with me.

CHAPTER 4

My eldest sister Sandra was growing up to be someone who couldn't control her emotions, whenever she had an argument with my mum she would end up saying the wrong things, or breaking things, or even releasing her anger on us. The house started to divide and Sandra's hatred towards Funmi and me grew more intense. I often questioned whether it was because we were from two different fathers.

Funmi, my sister from the same father, grew tough and took no nonsense, she alone challenged Sandra physically at times. Funmi started to get really protective of me, and at times she even got into physical fights with our mum, even slapping her face in defense of me. They would both fight until they got tired and then someone always left for the night to cool off.

I never did understand why my two sisters developed so much anger, but as they grew up I noticed others at school and outside the compound. The fights inside the house began to get bloody. The next time Funmi hit our mum, she was prepared. It happened so fast that before I knew it I saw my mum biting my sister around her hands and a little bit of her ears as well.

My sister kept screaming: "You fucking bitch, I hate you, I hope you die." That same night my sister was taken to the hospital for stitches. She didn't get time to properly heal, because as soon as she was stitched my mum had her officers lock her up in jail for further discipline. Funmi was locked up for a whole day and when she came out she looked terrible with bruises and mosquito bites covering her whole body. Whenever my mother got angry she no longer saw us as daughters from her womb, we became her enemies and she must destroy us in order to teach us a valuable lesson.

A couple years later, as Sandra became close to graduating from the University, she began planning her trip to move to the United States. Most parents believed it was better to do your schooling in

Nigeria before going off to make a living elsewhere because it gave the kids a better foundation of home training and discipline. I was beginning my secondary school level around the same time we started to plan Sandra's move to the USA. I must say it was a very sad and stressful experience for Sandra, as it was for any Nigerian preparing to go to America. It was tough because not only did she have to worry about passing the interview for the Visa but she also had to pay a huge amount of money for it. In those times bribery and corruption were very common, but unfortunately Sandra could not bribe her way into getting a Visa.

  The lady who interviewed her must have been having a bad day, because she denied her visa. The family was only in distress for a quick second. Just as we began to talk with her about planning a life in Nigeria, the idea came to us to ask my mum's younger sister, who was a well - travelled lady with an American passport, to let Sandra use it to enter the US. They had a very close resemblance, and it was a perfect idea, only my aunt was hesitant.

It took a long while to convince her of this plan, as she would need someone close to bring the passport safely back to her in Nigeria once Sandra was already in the US. While we waited for my aunt to agree Sandra continued looking for different ways to keep herself busy, half-believing that she would never be allowed to leave, after all it is a huge risk lending your passport out.

Chapter 5

I never really learned how to be a lady or what girls actually did for fun from the women in my family. I never knew how to wear bras, or leggings, or high heels. I didn't even know how to apply lip gloss, but I learned a little from watching movies and I truly learned it in my secondary school. I couldn't ask Funmi because she was a tomboy. I, on the other hand, was super feminine and was considered "aje butter," which meant someone who hardly faces hardships, hardly ever takes public transport, and has soft hands that looks like she has never washed dishes before.

Funmi, on the other hand, was a tough girl, and her friends were mostly boys that she played soccer with. Funmi never really liked skirts or dresses, which was a good thing as she had marks all over her legs from playing football and fighting, and they looked so bad that I was glad she stuck to mostly t-shirts and jeans. There was one day I even questioned her sexuality and his, I mean her, response was an immediate slap to my face that I never forgot.

I began my secondary education in a well-known school owned by the president of Nigeria at the time. My cousins Folarin and Folayo were already enrolled there, and that made things easier, but as I was in a separate part of the dormitory, I still had to figure out school life on my own.

As I dropped my school box onto my chosen bed, I heard from behind me: "O Girl! Don't put your box here, look for another bed - this bunk has been taken," and looked behind me to see who this was talking and it was a light skinned girl with the same straight, all-back braids as mine. Her face seemed aggressive, maybe because of the dirty looks she was giving me as she stood guarding her bed.

She had a beauty mark right by her lips, and I was looking at it trying to figure out if it was real or from an eye pencil when she spoke saying: "It be like, say this girl deaf: Oh, make una come help me Oh!"

As I started to reply to this feisty girl, another girl entered into the room saying: " Rukky, leave her now, nobody is sleeping under now."

Rukky: "Please leave this conversation, go and read for the English class test tomorrow before you start shelling and throwing bombs in the class."

Second Girl: "Oh please stop this nonsense! I don't shell (not properly using the right grammatical English terms) all the time. Just allow the girl to sleep in the under bed is all I know abeg." (abeg means please in Nigerian pidgin English)

Rukky: "Wait, don't tell me you are afraid because her mother is a police woman! You dey fear???!!!"

Second girl: "Abeg I no dey fear, the girl just land school nah, we can't be acting like Majesty college girls, acting all razz or local."

Rukky: "Look oh girl, I don't care who you are or what your mum is, me self my papa na army man, he will discipline your family."

I finally replied, "But what is all this for? If the bed is not taken, why can't I put my box dere?"

Rukky responded, "Babe because I don't want police woman daughter under me!"

I asked, "Where are you getting your news from self?"

Rukky answered, "It doesn't matter, everyone knows your mum is a police woman, the only thing that can help you now is if you drop chops (which means snacks in Nigerian pidgin English) for girls."

I replied, "which chops?"

Rukky: "Oh you won do like say we don't know you smuggled chops into the hostel."

Second girl: " God, fire your mouth Rukky why you dey attack this girl like this, you be agbero oh."

I spoke up, "So it's chops that's worrying you abi? oya don't worry, let me take this bed. I'll settle you later."

Rukky: "will you drop chops police daughter, in fact what's your name?"

I replied, "I'm Funke Adedayo."

Second Girl: "nice to meet you, better person."

Rukky: "Is she talking to you? Abeg go back to Green House you are disturbing us, this is YELLOW HOUSE!!!"

Rukky screamed, then continued: "I'm Rukky, don't mind me, I was just checking if you were tough to challenge the other girls."

The second girl made a "hmmm" sound, then said " her name is Rukiat and she is our classmate, don't let her be talking to you anyhow." As they continued to argue playfully, I just knew they both would be my good friends in the secondary school.

Chapter 6

In most schools the dormitories were separated by colors which were also used for the inter-house sports events that included marching, running, and other Olympic-style activities. There were four major houses, or colors, that all students fell into: yellow, red, blue, and green. You didn't have a choice in the matter, the department that gave you your uniform and textbooks usually just handed whatever color they could reach over to you. The dinner hall was huge, and was where both boarding and day students met for meals.

Most of the students lived at the school because their parents either couldn't afford the cost of fuel to drive them every day or were just too busy to watch over them. In the boarding houses usually the last Sunday of each month was a visiting day. The parents would come from all over to bring provisions, more money, and just simply to see their child. In a boarding house setting it was smart to make friends with the cooks, so that whenever there was a meal you truly hated they could cook you something special on the side, or give you two pieces of chicken instead of one.

    Secondary school life was intense. The punishments were crazy: you could be asked to kneel down with a chair on your head, to pick up a pencil with one leg stretched out in the air, to dig your height with a shovel, or even to wash the school dishes for all 2,000 students.

    Rukky and Oyinkan became my very close friends, and they often visited me back home in Aguda when my mother wasn't around. We stuck together even through the toughest times in school, we usually got in trouble together and were punished together. We were a clique and we sat together during classes unless the instructors separated us. I experienced my first time physical fight with Rukky, and it was over a boy. Sometimes I would wake up to find that my hair had been cut with scissors. I knew it couldn't be Rukky, but it was typical that the other girls who were jealous of our friendship would do anything to tear us apart.

    I experienced my first Social Night when my friends and I were promoted to SS1(Senior Secondary School 1). Social Night was when all the students got together to engage in activities like games, dancing, and movie nights. Social night pretty much turned me into a full woman -once I was finally allowed to take off my uniform, I started getting male attention. I learned how to properly apply makeup, and wear clothes with high slits and deep V-necks to show my cleavage. It was then that I gave thanks to Rukky and Oyinkan for teaching me the wonders of a push-up bra! My breasts were large in size and putting them on display in a push-up bra drove the boys wild!

    I was quite daring in my class, I usually launched the trendy clothes: the hipsters, pedal pushers, and spaghetti-tops I got from my cousins who travelled a lot and knew all the latest styles.

The school uniform didn't allow the boys to properly visualize the girl's natural assets, so they always looked forward to Social Night.

Social Night was when boys got free "quaves," which is Nigerian slang for lap dances or close encounters while dancing. It was also a night where some girls got their dirty wishes answered: you would see them in dark corners being fingered or raising up their skirts for easier access, and the boys would slightly pull down their pants to quickly hammer that hungry hole right before the house masters came back to watch us.

It's a sad fact that the boys who committed these acts would be praised while the girls they banged were labeled secondary school sluts. Once you were known as the school slut, every horny boy would head in your direction: even the lames, and nerds, and seniors who wanted a junior slut to test their manhood with.

Chapter 7

Whenever Funmi and I were back home from school it seemed as if my mother was the only one happy to see us. Sandra seemed distant, and would often stay at a friend's place or in her room so as not to be bothered. Funmi didn't notice but I did. I felt the distance between us, and it was starting to become obvious that we were from different fathers.

This period was also filled with some of the best moments of my life: attending, along with my cousins, every happening party thrown by the students of our school. Back then, even if you didn't have an invitation, if you were a girl you would still get in.

During this time I was constantly getting whoopings from my mum and siblings for coming home extremely late, wearing inappropriate clothing, wearing my sister's clothes without their consent, and sometimes just for going to parties in the first place. I should have listened to them and toned down on the partying, because little did I know a major scar was coming my way.

One weekend I followed my cousins and Funmi to a music festival at TB Square (Tafawa Balewa Square). One by one, obstacles kept cropping up that seemed they would prevent us from going: first the driver couldn't make it into work that day, then there wasn't enough space in the car, then there wasn't enough money for a taxi. Finally, out of nowhere, the money was provided by my grandma when she saw how upset we were.

Finally, we were on our way: looking fabulous, sexy, and appetizing. The TB Square was a huge building named after Nigeria's first prime minister. Tafawa Balewa is situated in the center of Lagos, and often hosts the EYO masquerade festival, music festivals, and many more celebrations. As we got down from the taxicab, we saw a large crowd of people heading into the arena. The girls were almost naked, and clearly on a mission to show off what they were working with, and it started to feel like there were more women than men.

Soon the music started and people began dancing all around the arena. It was a fun-filled place to be, and the only downside was encountering girls from school I didn't like, and the occasional fights that broke out when people were breaking bottles and getting rowdy.

Eventually it started to get late, and the DJ cut off the music as everyone's clue to started heading out. We started to pack up, exchange numbers, and head towards the entrance. As soon as we stepped outside the TB Square gate, it was chaos. I heard the sound of a gunshot, and right in front of my eyes our group scattered.

All I could see was Funmi fighting a guy who was reaching out to grab the chain she was wearing. For a few minutes I stayed frozen out of fear, and it wasn't until I moved into a gutter that I was noticed. Suddenly I saw two guys standing over me, and for a second I thought they were trying to help me out of the gutter, but then they both started to pull on my shirt. I fought back, and it wasn't easy fighting both of them at once.

Finally, they ripped off my t-shirt which was a designer t shirt, and then one stayed back to try to pull off my bra. At first, I thought he wanted to try and sell it, but it quickly became obvious he was trying to feel my breasts, or even rape me. I felt like i was going to die, tears were rolling down my eyes and I was screaming for help, but the sounds of all the other girls in need of help overpowered mine and it got lost behind the sounds of all the cars speeding by.

There were no police officers in sight, and there were many girls fighting for their lives. I was getting weak and ready to give in, I couldn't fight much longer. I pleaded with him to stop but he wasn't listening. He was high on drugs - sweating and salivating like some sort of dog ready to devour a bone.

Just then I saw two guys approach the back of my attacker and began swinging sticks against his head. As I stood up to recover myself, all I saw was my attacker passed out on the floor and the two rescuers gone! They had vanished like angels.

My shirt was still in my attacker's hands, and as I grabbed it away from him I noticed that one of my bra straps was torn. Once I started to come back to myself, I looked over just in time to see my cousin get hit in the face by a golf club from her own attacker. I screamed from shock and ran towards her to help as he ran off with the rest of his gang.

I scanned her face to see where exactly the golf club had hit her, and breathed a sigh of relief that it was only her lips - it could have been so much worse. Carefully I pulled her up towards the streets and away from the crowd. Once we had found a safe spot, we glanced back only to see the police cars finally arriving after it was all over. The remaining attackers ran as soon as they saw the police officers, but they didn't run empty-handed. We watched as they lifted a thick girl right above their heads running and shooting pistols into the air in delight. No one knew the girl they carried away, but we all knew she would be badly raped by all the gang members and probably shot.

Once we all regained consciousness, we jumped into a random cab, sitting on each other's laps this time instead of taking two separate cars. The ride home to Aguda was silent, no one said a word. Everyone was worn out, tired, and out of breath. The only sound came from my cousin who was moaning in pain from her swollen lips. I did a quick scan around the car and noticed Funmi's chain was gone and she had lots of scratch marks on her neck. Fortunately, my younger cousins were fine compared to the rest of us.

That night was very scary and afterwards I didn't want to attend a gathering anywhere in Lagos where unknown people would be attending. I couldn't stop thinking about the girl they took away to rape and wondering if the way we had dressed and behaved had helped to seduce the devils.

In Nigeria we were taught that wearing a short skirt or dress and a cleavage-revealing top could be construed as an invitation to rape and harassment, but we did it anyway because it was hip, and we wanted to be the talk of the party. But then I thought to myself that women should be allowed to wear whatever they wanted without being forced into things they didn't agree to. Why must we walk in fear of being raped every time we step into the streets of Lagos or anywhere else? Would a rapist consider it acceptable for another man to rape his own mother or sister?

Once a woman is raped, she is automatically traumatized, She will carry it with her for the rest of her life, seeing his face in her dreams. The memories will stick with her and could even keep her from responding to the love of her life if his every touch feels like the touch of the man that raped her.

In a place like Nigeria the most that a rape victim got was family members and friends saying "Sorry," or "The Lord will take care of things," and "That's enough, please stop thinking about it." Girls were constantly blamed for the clothes they wore and the time they went out, until it got to the point that they blamed themselves as well. She was the reason the man got tempted, she was supposed to be aware that men are unable to control themselves.

When a boy gets raped he is called weak for allowing it and not using his manly strength to push the woman off him. He may even be told it was a blessing that the woman chose him to rape - the fact that she climbed him, and he was able to get his penis inserted in her for free was considered a gift, as long as she was good looking.

In places like Nigeria there weren't any private centers where you could go and talk about your rape to begin to heal from the mental and emotional damage. No form of assistance was ever advertised on radio or television, or even talked about.

Chapter 8

After a few months, we graduated from secondary school. Then we just had to wait for our parents to decide whether we would continue our schooling at home in Nigeria, or abroad in London or America. The decision was finally made for me to go to the US, and it was an easy one because not only had I received an acceptance letter, but my sister Sandra was already living in the States. My mum thought things would be easier if I went to stay with Sandra, but she was concerned that she wouldn't have enough money for both me and Funmi to go at the same time.

Funmi wasn't really excited about going to America, so she suggested I go first and that she would come much later. I thought this was the most foolish decision I had ever heard. No one I knew would give up their space to travel to the United States for someone else. Even though we fought a lot, I knew Funmi loved me deeply and felt responseble for me. The decision for her to give up her place for me to go to America first was shocking, and I hugged her upon hearing the good news. I didn't really pack many of my clothes, as I planned to get new and better ones like they wore in American music videos. I took only a few things that would remind me of home, and some photos albums to look at when I got lonely.

It was my first time going to the Muritala Mohammed International Airport, and it was an interesting journey. Living in Lagos I had no idea what the Third Mainland Bridge was until I finally saw it. The Third Mainland Bridge was the longest bridge in all of Africa - 11.8 km in length. The traffic could take up to one or two hours to get across. If you didn't have a clear idea of where you were going, you would definitely get lost as the road signs were no help. Many of the signs had fallen down and the traffic officials hadn't ever fixed it, so you usually had to ask around for directions, while taking care not to ask the armed robbers who lurked by the roadside.

There was so much traffic outside of the airport, that it often came to a full stop, and the people would have to get down from their cars to carry their luggage on their head the final few blocks to the airport doors. There were soldiers at the departure gate who prevented people who weren't actually traveling from entering, so Funmi couldn't come in with me.

During the flight I kept busy making a long list of all the things I wanted to do: school, modeling, and dozens of other pursuits, and by the end of the 18 hour flight I was exhausted. When we reached the customs there were two lines, one for U.S. citizens, and one for visitors. I was pulled aside for inspection, and as the officer directed me to another line he shouted to the officer I was walking towards: "Nigerian Number 12." I didn't know what that meant, but I guess we had made a mark that day during their shift. On finally reaching the street, I waited and waited for about 45 minutes before a man finally parked in front of me. He got out of the car and walked up to me calling my name.

    Once he saw the look of confusion on my face he immediately introduced himself as Sandra's husband Tokunbo. Apparently, my sister had to work that day and couldn't call off. It was very awkward as I'd only spoken to him over the phone and we had never met in person. We rode in silence all the way from the airport.

    Once we arrived, he showed me to my room which was cold and lacking a bed. They hadn't prepared at all for my arrival, and that night I slept on the bare carpet and just threw all my clothes on top of myself to keep warm. When my sister arrived she gave me a lecture about how to behave: to not ever enter her bedroom unless she told me to, to dress appropriately in front of her husband so as not to seduce him, and to not invite friends over in her absence because she had jewelry laying around.

    Once I washed my underwear and hung it in the bathroom to dry, and she responded by embarrassing me in front of her husband, throwing the panties on my head and telling me to get an American guide book and learn about laundromats. She eventually bought a blow-up bed for me to use, but after a few days it went bad and flat. I had made promises with my old friends Rukky and Oyinkan to stay in contact no matter what, but when life set its hardships on me I just couldn't keep those promises anymore.

Chapter 9

The United States turned out to be exactly the same as it was in the movies. The environment was much cleaner, the streets were perfectly done, the buildings were tall and well-constructed, and the shopping centers were very inviting. Life was totally different, and I wanted to blend in smoothly. I didn't want to be seen as an African girl, so I made sure to pay attention to what everyone my age was wearing. I mimicked how they talked, the food they ate, and how they dressed. I was living with my sister on the North Side of Chicago which seemed to be mostly Caucasians. You see Chicago, apart from being terribly cold during winter, had a high crime rate and was very segregated. The whites lived Downtown and on the North Side, the Asians lived in Chinatown, the Blacks lived on the South Side, and the Mexicans on the West Side. Africans seemed to be mainly on the North and South suburbs.

Sandra warned me about the Africans who were being pressured by their families to get married, so that whenever they saw a fresh new girl from Africa they would be all over her. She told me a lot about life in Chicago. We talked about the Nigerians who came to the States with advanced degrees and education only to end up as a taxi driver or security guards or even home health aides. Most Nigerians worked as nurses or in the health department, as it was the best way to make quick money to support their family back at home. Sandra taught me how to use the CTA Transit by myself, but the map they gave me never really worked so I just ventured into the streets and figured it out on my own.

    I couldn't start school just yet as it was past the application deadline and I had to wait for the next semester. In the meantime, I looked for a job to keep myself busy, but it seemed like no one wanted to hire someone like myself who had no retail experience. It would have been nice for Sandra to let me know to have a resume at hand when going to these stores, or even that resume was the same thing we called a CV in Nigeria.

In Nigeria, you had to complete a NYSC (National Youth Service Corps) program after you had finished with your university level before you could legally work. The purpose of the NYSC program was to teach young people how to serve the community of Nigeria before they went on to become her future leaders. Students were shuffled around in different states for this, although those with connections were able to bribe their way into staying in their own city, or to have the officials sign them in and out on a daily basis while they travelled around. The program lasted for a full year and I thought of it as a prison camp. It seemed scary that you could easily be sent to a high crime state that you had never been to before, and there was nothing you could do to complain, in fact you would be considered weak for complaining.

Some students were even killed while serving at the NYSC camp in certain states. Not killed directly in the camp of course, but often if they ventured out to go to a party or explore the city. Many young men were killed in hotel rooms by prostitutes who worked alongside ritualists. The youth's head would then be cut off and used in a wealth ritual for a man in need of a better life for his family. In the movies it was an admirable thing to see a high school kid both working and going to school, because we weren't allowed to do so in Nigeria.

Finally, I dropped my pride and approached a lady who seemed to be the manager of a store to ask her in my most straight forward manner what a beginner had to do to get a job.

Me: "I'm sorry to bother you, but I have no idea how it works when you are applying for a job in the United States."

Manager: "Well for starters, it is always best to introduce yourself."

Me: "Oh, I am sorry, my name is Funke Adedayo."

Manager: "Nice to meet you Funke, I'm Kimberly. Where are you from? You have an accent and your name is different."

Me: "I'm from Nigeria."

Manager: "Oh Nigeria!!! Like Lagos, Nigeria?"

Me: "Yes Lagos, Nigeria."

Manager: "I mean no offense, but your men are very aggressive, my God!"

I laughed then, and said, "Why do you say that? Have you dated one?"

Manager: "Yes I have my gosh, and he was crazy, always asking where I was after I got off work!"

Me: "I'm sure he just wanted to know you were safe."

Manager: "You know he just wanted to be in control, even though he did pay most of my bills, so I guess I couldn't complain too much. It was a fresh breath of air compared to American men who don't do much but buy Air Jordans for themselves, won't even give you a dollar and expect sex after they get off work."

Me: "I couldn't compare the two, I haven't dated an American black man yet."

Manager: "Let me tell you in advance - don't even bother - there's nothing to expect from them other than sex - you're better off dating white men."

Let's just say Kimberly taught me everything I needed to know except for the real reason I came to her store, which was to learn how to properly apply for a job. Much later she did eventually teach me about the proper ways to apply for a job, interview, and follow up after the interview.

Initially I thought my sister Sandra was interested in my well-being and concerned that I stay on right path to start my future in Chicago. As the weeks went on however, she began to complain all the time. She complained about my use of her phone, reminding me that I didn't have a job to help pay the bill; she complained to my mum that I didn't help much around the house, but what she really wanted was for me to babysit her kids rather than get a job in the real world.

Instead of my mother calling to find out how I was dealing with all of this, she called and asked for me to refund the ticket money that had brought me to Chicago. It wasn't as if she didn't have any money, in fact she was in the process of building a new home. I was very saddened by her selfishness, but I couldn't express myself because in my culture we were taught that our parents were always right. So instead, I decided to just ignore her calls and take a break from talking to her.

Eventually I found myself babysitting after all simply to keep peace in the house and be able to eat properly. Otherwise I would have been denied food and pushed out to job search with no way to get back in the house until she returned from work and picked her kids up from school. The one time I tried to refuse babysitting she instructed her husband not to let me in if he returned home before she did.

Chapter 10

Sandra was ruthless, she treated me more like a maid than a sister. There was one day I didn't wash the dishes and I didn't get the kids in bed by 7pm, and when she got home around 8 she questioned me on why the kids weren't in bed.

I wanted to apologize, but before I could utter a word I was whacked across the face with a slap. At age 19 my senior sister slapped me, all because her kids weren't in bed by the designated time. When she slapped me I wondered how to respond: should I give her a slap in return, should I walk out with my belongings, where would I go? I was trapped with no friends and no other family members within the neighborhood to go to.

Close to a year went by living in that house and I still hadn't registered for classes. My sister Funmi knew I couldn't possibly go to school with so much negative energy in the house, but according to my mother I was wasting my life away. Sandra agreed with my mother, but really, she just enjoyed saving money by having me as a babysitter.

I hoped Sandra's husband Tokunbo would help her have a change of heart toward what I needed to be doing in the US. I had conversations with him whenever he was home, and I noticed his way of thinking was different than his wife. He seemed open to people, and like someone who kept a regular, decent, legal job.

The truth was that he was a dealer, a fraud, one of those Nigerians who give the rest of us a bad name. Tokunbo was a socialite within the Nigerian community. He attended all the concerts and club parties and dressed to kill in designer fashions. For a while I wondered how someone with no 9 - 5 job could afford such outfits. One day when I, as the current help, was doing the laundry, I came across numerous credit cards with all different names like Susie Chan, Robert Crane, and Samson Foster.

He would often have six different cards at

once. Tokunbo would use the credit cards to shop and have the shipment come to a particular address at a certain time. Other times he would have a friend who worked at a retail shop steal some clothing and pass it to him in the parking lot.

They pretended as though they were throwing out the garbage and would stuff new clothing into the garbage can, push it outside, and from there Tokunbo would take it and put it in his car trunk to sell. I do think he used part of the money he stole to buy toys for his kids and clothes for Sandra, but I was doing everything possible to stay away from him, as I feared that one day the police would break in and take everyone who was present into custody for the fraudulent activities he had committed.

The one time he tried to talk to my sister concerning my schooling, she immediately accused me of trying to seduce her husband and threaten her marriage. They started arguing over my schooling, his motives were truly innocent, but Sandra assumed it was just because he was interested in taking me to bed. I wondered if this had happened before with someone else who stayed with them.

Chapter 11

Out of nowhere I was confronted with the saddest news of my life - my sister Funmi had died. Funmi had sickle cell anemia and got sick a lot when we were kids. I never really understood it, but I wish now that I had had a better understanding of her medical condition. I think it would have had me cherish her more and truly appreciate the days we had together.

I would have gladly given my place for her to come to the US first because if she got sick here it would have been handled professionally and properly. My mother told me that Funmi had grown very ill, was breathing hard, and hadn't eaten for a whole day. She said Funmi was finally admitted to the hospital after extensive arguments with the doctors and nurses. Nigerians strongly believe in the concept of "Pay before Service." It is mostly associated with prostitutes, but it is also used by medical doctors. They wanted to receive full payment up front before even begin-

-ning her treatment. My mother told me she put on her police uniform and begged on her knees to get them to start treatment, but they refused. She had to run all the way home to gather the requested funds, but by the time she returned so much time had already been lost.

My mum started to see the signs that they were losing Funmi and left to go get the pastor. While she was gone, the untrained nurse chose to put Funmi on a drip rather than alerting my mother to bring someone who could donate blood. Funmi was gone by the time she returned. My mother blamed herself for leaving, and in Nigeria you can't sue the hospital. Even if we could, no amount of money could relieve the pain of a mother standing over her dead daughter.

I became numb, my soul frozen with ice cubes of pain and sorrow. My childhood memories flashed before my eyes and tears rolled down my face. At that moment I wanted to give up on everything. Receiving sad news is one thing, but not having anyone to share it with or lean on and cry for a bit is even more painful.

i was present physically but mentally absent. I was bumping into people as I walked, dropping things I found it hard to carry, and standing alone. All that I watched and all that I saw reminded me of Funmi, I couldn't think straight or think of anything other than her. Even when it was time for her funeral I couldn't go, I was trapped in Chicago. I entered the US with a visiting visa which was close to expiring, and I knew if I had gone home for Funmi's funeral I may not have been able to return to America.

My mum attended the funeral with just my aunts, her driver, and two other people making a total of six altogether. In our tradition a young person's funeral was kept extremely private, in fact her name wasn't even inscribed on the tombstone so it really was the last time you would be able to say goodbye, as there was no way to come back later and find her unmarked tombstone.

Sandra didn't seem as hurt by the news as much as my mother and I. You may think I am only saying this because of the rocky moments I was experiencing in her house, but there were times when I cried late into the night, just lying there and thinking of Funmi. Sandra would walk in and tell me to shut up and stop disturbing her kids rather than comfort me. One time she said, "Would you shut up and stop crying like you're the first person to lose a sister? Please don't wake up my children, they are starting school tomorrow," and shut the door. Those were the words of someone who cared for Funmi I guess, but how Sandra got so cold is just a mystery to me.

That night I remember I wrote a piece in my diary for Funmi. I didn't put any title, I just wrote like I was going to send it as a letter to her in the heavens.

In a place so dark I fall to the floor. My chest hurts like I have been pierced with a long sword. We were just planning for you to come to the United States of America. Now we are at a point where I find it hard to breathe, did I wait too long to insist that you come to the US? I could have sacrificed my time to make sure you were brought here sooner. I could have waited to come with you at the same time. Everything I have is nothing without my sister by my side. With pain I sleep in regret, I rest my head. In anger I take these pills, in fear I don't think I can continue living. In my mind I keep your heavenly face frozen with a smile that reminds me of reasons to stay alive as you would want me to.

I wanna say you have taught me so much within the little time I've known you as a person. You were much more than my sister to me. You were my guardian, without your presence I feel scared but I wouldn't do you proud if I for a second became weak. People say "Let the Lord handle things, whether it be little or big." You always told me to think outside the box, that certain situations could be solved by just asking another human being.

You taught me that Heaven helps those who help themselves, so that's why I always did my best on Earth and prayed right along as I waited for the Lord to respond. If I was present at your farewell funeral I would have held your hand while I talked to you. I would want to be buried with you because you have always known that no one in our family really gave a damn about me as you did. Right now, I feel like I am going to have fight constantly till I die with the rest of our family. Truthfully, I have no one to fight this battle with me.

    Can you open the doors to Heaven, so I can escape living in a place called Hell with a family portrait filled with lies? You once told me I should save my tears for a day when I really would need them. I guess this day has finally presented itself as you have left me. I remember when our mother struck me with her kitten heels because I yelled to see our dad and then you charged and threw them back at her. You have always been protective of me, how do I continue fighting this battle still present in my life? I'm here crying both of our tears, I know in Heaven you are doing nothing but smiling, so that's why here on Earth I'm crying your tears for you because I know there was so much you had planned to do. I wonder if anyone, any human, will come to love me like you do my sister.

My soul bleeds every time I hear your name, my tears can't be held back, not even if I tried my hardest. When I look at our family albums I cut it, leaving me and only you. They say we should cherish our days because no one knows tomorrow. The heavens have taken you from me, but I know there is a greater mission up there, way better than what you had planned on earth. So, I say watch over me my sister. Guide me when I'm about to go astray. Tell the angels to run to me when I am need of protection from the evil ones. Tell the Lord our story, and now my story, so he can forgive me and my future sins.

After I wrote this piece I closed my diary and went to bed crying all through the night until I finally fell asleep for a few minutes.

Chapter 12

Once I started to gain some strength to continue life after dealing with the loss of my sister I started to strategize on how I could better myself without any support. I decided that if my sister Sandra was going to act like this I should be making money for myself. Mainly because I needed to pay for school processing, but I was also worried she may not want to help with female products for my personal hygiene. I went to Michigan Ave in downtown Chicago to fill out applications. The lady Kimberly, who I had met a couple of weeks prior, taught me about how to dress, how to present yourself when asking for an application, and how to create a resume. To her credit, she never told me about lying on your resume. But she did say sometimes you have to fake it till you make it, so yes, I lied on my resume, I mentioned stores in London that had closed down so that if they needed to verify employment, it wouldn't be possible and it would be left to my personality, interview skills, and communication. I have to say I did a fine job during the interview, I walked out confident that I had been given the position, even though I was told to wait until Monday for a reply. I didn't have a personal phone at the time, so I had left my sister's number for the contact.

Monday finally arrived, and I was kinda happy Sandra didn't go out that day otherwise I wouldn't have been able to share the good news. Around 3:45 pm the phone started to ring, and when I looked over I immediately recognized the number. I had no idea where Sandra was, so I picked up the phone and said "Hello!" Sandra came out of her room screaming, "Are you mad?!"

I replied, "What happened, what's wrong?" she then replied "Are you helping me pay the phone bill? Who asked you to pick up my calls?" As I struggled to respond she snatched the phone out of my hand and started to speak. I heard her shout, "You have the wrong number, there's no one by the name Funke on this line, thank you!" and hung up. Reeling from shock I asked, "Why would you say that? That's the place I went to interview."

She responded, "Will you shut up, when you decided to buy McDonalds and eat outside, wasting money here and there, why didn't you also buy a phone to receive calls on?" I usually had a smart response for my sister when she decided to act crazy like this, but that day I had nothing to say, I was just actually lost.

I was still determined to work and afford the things I wanted and hopefully at some point move to an environment where I could enjoy my independence. So, the next day I went over to the store I had interviewed at to find out if I had gotten the job. I was given the bad news that because I was not able to be reached, they had given the position to the next qualified candidate on the list. The manager did say if something else opened up they would call me, but while she was speaking I felt so much anger building up in me - mentally revisiting how my sister picked up the phone and told them I do not exist as I stood there beside her. It's sad to be in a situation with no support system whatsoever. If I had been able to save anything from Nigeria I would have started to look for somewhere else to live, but I was stuck with little to nothing saved and no idea of where to go.

Chapter 13

Over the weeks I started to get involved in the church activities: attending every event, night vigils, and both morning and evening services. I knew practically half of the congregation, the pastor, the kids, even the security guards that helped with parking. I should back up and say that I am a Christian, but sometimes I believed in resting and praying at home, I knew God would still answer my prayers. So truthfully, it was my sister who forced me out of the house on Sundays. Whenever I wanted to stay home, she would threaten me saying: "Well you cannot stay in my house, I serve the Lord and everyone under my roof should do the same or leave my Holy presence with their evil state of mind." I had no option but to force myself out of the house - even when I was sick she would say: "If you are sick, it's all the more reason why you need to receive prayer in the house of the Lord and be healed, get in the car and let's go."

Even though Sandra enforced Christianity in her house her husband Tokunbo was a Muslim, but I wouldn't dare bring this to her attention. My sister and the pastor further ambushed me into being an usher, telling me that: "Serving the Lord in his house will create open doors for you to work elsewhere to get funds." I'm pretty sure the pastor had no idea that I had already received an offer but my sister had destroyed and burnt that flag of success.

In the eyes of the church members Sandra was the responsible sister who was looking out for me and I was the wayward one who needed guidance. I had to watch what I said around the other ushers because I was pretty sure they were the eyes and ears of the pastor within the church.

Churches in general had become gossip residences and you learned to keep your secrets and problems to yourself or risk them being discussed in the private homes of the church members, or worse, used to preach about on a Sunday morning.

I was doing as Sandra wanted: serving the Lord and

playing the role of faithful usher in the church. At home I was a standby babysitter who was paid only in insults, dirty looks, and enough negative memories to last me the whole Christmas season. I remember trying to apply for a scholarship thinking that if I won it I could use the money towards school and get an apartment. The scholarship application was supposed to be an essay about current societal problems that needed to be brought to attention around Chicago. I decided instead to make it a confessional letter about my living situation, thinking this would help me either get the scholarship or get someone to come help me before I started to consider suicide.

  Just when I thought things were at their worst, I discovered it was only the beginning of the madness I would endure . On many occasions I would find myself having crazy conversations with Tokunbo, Sandra's husband, he kept asking me if I was having sex, and every time he brought it up I would shut the topic down with a firm no and then act like I was busy cleaning or cooking. The next time he would come back even more aggressively, telling me that I shouldn't waste my body and should make sure I was collecting money for my favors, that nobody with a great body would just lay down and give free sex under the guise of love.

Tokunbo: "You have big breasts, and I'm sure all the Nigerian commissioners and chiefs would be wiring money to you here. You need to be smart girl."

Me: "I know, but I am not that kind of girl. I want to be rich through all of the hard work I am putting in."

Tokunbo: "You can be so daft at times, the only 100 percent work you are putting in is being a slave for your sister."

Me: "That's your wife, you should advise her to help me find a job."

Tokunbo: "You should want fast money, not money with taxes that will frustrate you when you collect the check. Girl you are not sharp."

Me: "I am fine thank you, God will provide work and I will keep searching."

Tokunbo: "You know what to do when you are ready, in fact I have rich friends that will pamper you, and you don't even need to work anymore in your life, just be a housewife. You will thank me for this, I promise you."

Me: "Is that the kind of friends you keep? Wow!"

Tokunbo: "Yes, very rich friends, who needs to be associated with broke ass mother fuckers?"

Me: "No I'm good, thank you."

Tokunbo: "In fact, I can test the car myself before my friends do. Just to make sure you are capable of handling them. Nobody has to know. We will use condom, oh, we have to be smart, no more babies for me."

Me: " EXCUSE YOU! YOU ARE MY UNCLE, I WILL NEVER!!!"

Tokunbo: "I am just joking! Argh, calm down, I was just trying to see if you were the loose type, but I am glad you reacted that way. What kind of person do you take me for? I would never do such a thing."

I was so shocked at the way he boasted and spoke. The suggestions he made to me were disgusting, and I couldn't tell Sandra because I know her reaction would be over the roof. She would never believe what I told her, I would probably just get a slap for my trouble. Sometimes he would even come home from a party with his friends and bring one over to me in the kitchen to introduce us.

Tokunbo: "Hey, this is my wife's little sister."

Friend: "Wow she is fine, right packing from God also."

Me: "Umm . . . Hi?"

Tokunbo: "OK, I'll leave you two adults to talk while I go chill with the guys."

Friend: "So, he tells me you are looking for a boyfriend to take care of you."

Me: "I never told him that."

Friend: "Are you shy?"

Me: "I am not shy, I am just irritated."

Friend: "What's wrong? Am I ugly?"

Me: "Mista, I don't know you and I'm not that kind of girl, please."

Friend: "I have plenty money, I have a good job, good looking as you can see, I'm single, big dick and give great sex. What else does a woman need?"

Me: "I can care less what you have, but when a woman is handed over like a prostitute when she is not one then she must take charge and dismiss the fools doing this trade by barter business."

Friend: "Did you just call me a fool?"

Me: "Yes I did, in fact you should be ashamed of yourself."

Friend: "Abeg stop there, all you Naija girls come here acting like you are grand but are leftover packages. You are not even happy a guy like myself is taking time to invest in your poor background."

I walked away before he could continue to speak and headed towards the living room where Tokunbo was. I wanted to get him to come warn his friend before I ended up swinging at him with a frying pan but I was very surprised at what I saw. The table was covered with drinks, cigarettes, and dollar bills in stacks, and Tokunbo had what seemed to be a white substance all around his nose area. He and his friends were lowering their heads into a paper with more of the white substance. I knew what it was immediately, even though he dragged me away quickly and tried his best to give it any other name than cocaine.

At that moment I realized that he must have expected his friend to win me over with his words in the kitchen which would have given them enough time to sniff all of the cocaine in secrecy. I knew now that I was no longer safe and could possibly be in serious danger with all this going on around me. I wasn't sure if Sandra knew, and I didn't have a phone to take pictures for proof.

Then I stopped myself - what if she already knew the kind of guy she was with and I was just going to be the barking dog disturbing their drugs and perfect relationship. That night I called my mum to tell her what I had seen, I just had to speak to someone. My mum didn't want to believe it, and I told her not to tell Sandra until I could get more proof. I told her I needed her to help me find someone else's house to stay in so that I could feel safer. My mum promised to find someone and to keep hush about what I had seen in Sandra's house that day.

Chapter 14

I was starting to learn that many American families believed it was a normal thing to throw a child out of the house once they came of age. I had always considered it to be cruel, but I never expected I would experience it myself. When that day came, it was random, and I wasn't expecting it. I remember laying down in my room, taking advantage of the quiet and peaceful environment. I had wondered all day where the kids were, totally clueless that there was a plan being executed.

Suddenly Sandra burst through my bedroom door, and before I could even take the blanket off my face she kicked me extremely hard. I grabbed the side of my stomach in pain as she yelled: "I heard all you've been telling mum about how I'm treating you like a house maid and that you've been suffering, you also told her we do drugs in this house, well you will now enjoy yourself with your freedom but not in my house!".

I replied, "I didn't say anything like that, mum must have taken it to another level," but before I could finish speaking she blessed me with her hands across my face. She pulled me out of bed aggressively, pushing me towards the living room where her husband was sitting at the dining table eating a burger and acting like he didn't see what was happening.

I stood there embarrassed in my night robe, wondering where Sandra had gone, as she had headed back into my room. In another instant she was rushing towards me with a heap of clothes which seemed to be mine. She threw them over my head yelling "GET OUT OF MY HOUSE!!!" Immediately I fell on my knees begging and crying for forgiveness, I still wasn't sure what I had done that was so wrong she couldn't even have a conversation with her blood sister.

Sandra threw my boxes and all my toiletries towards me, continuing to yell as she flung them out the door into the cold. I remember it was snowing, and I begged her husband to plead with her, but all he did was lift his hands and say, "That's between you and your crazy family, you went to tell the whole of Nigeria that I do drugs? Leave me alone please." After Sandra had succeeded in throwing out all my things, she threatened to call the cops if I didn't leave peacefully. I was still on the floor weeping and pleading then she started to slap me and beat me all over, even trying to humiliate me by pulling open the string on my robe. I struggled for a while not expose my nakedness, and then finally gave up and walked myself down the stairs to the main door and cried right on the doorstep in the freezing cold. I remembered my hands stiffening and finding it hard to move my fingers as I stood there watching my clothes slowly being covered with the snow.

    After a few minutes of waiting for death, I had the random idea to run down to the doughnut store hoping they might help me out or I could at least keep warm while I thought of my next step. I gathered all my clothes into the box, shoved them to the side, and ran straight there with my feet bare on the cold, wet, slippery ground.

My feet felt numb totally frozen, like they could break into blocks of ice, but I ran towards the store with no delay.

When I finally reached the doughnut store I saw that it closed at midnight and it was already 11:50 pm. My hopes were dashed when the cleaner met me by the door and said very aggressively: "We are closed!"

I replied that the sign said open until midnight. She remained by the entrance, blocking my way and telling me that even though the sign said midnight, it was technically 11:45pm when they closed the doors and stopped the customers from entering so that they could close the registers. All this while she could clearly see the tears rolling down my eyes and that I was barefoot and wearing only a night robe.

As I tried to tell her my story she cut me off halfway saying, "Sorry, we cannot help you, this is clearly not a police station, it's a doughnut store." She continued to joke, laughing rudely and shouting, "Sorry miss, doughnuts can't help you with whatever you're going through." I took a few steps back and my eyes got blurry with teardrops, I turned in embarrassment and ran back to the front of my sister's house.

I have heard people saying God sometimes sends someone to your life at a particular juncture to help guide you through a tough trial. That day a random man was standing in front of our house looking through the mail boxes, and as I walked up to him he looked startled and stared me up and down before asking what had happened to me. He told me he used to live upstairs for about 3 years and that his name was Mark. I explained to him what had just happened, and immediately he gave me his phone to call the police, especially once I told him that my passport and all my documents were still in the house.

It took about five calls and an hour and half before the police finally arrived - by then I was sitting in Mark's taxi car. The police came to the front of the house, and I stepped out of his car to walk towards them. As I started to explain, the male officer (whose name was Derrick) cut me off and didn't let me finish my story.

He headed to the door, knocked, and entered the house. Gradually more police officers arrived at the scene, I guess Derrick had asked for backup. All I could think was maybe Sandra had refused to explain why she threw me out and he had decided to arrest her, and she was resisting arrest.

I didn't necessarily want her to be arrested, I only wanted some more time to stay before I had to move out, as Mark had advised me to say when the cops had arrived. I tried to tell the female cop this, but she just told me to put down my purse and anything else I was holding, and as I was doing so I noticed Sandra crying and walking out with Derrick the officer.

He wasn't holding her or trying to arrest her, but she did seem frightened and tears were falling down her eyes. I had no idea what was going on, I was lost, and when the cops told me to turn around I just cried "Why?!"

The officer replied saying, "Ma'am, please just turn around!" As I continued to try and explain, he forced me to turn around and I saw that metal thing that I had only seen in the movies. The handcuffs were placed on my hands, and as I felt the metal against my skin I had a flashback and zoned out for a little while.

It wasn't the first time I had had cuffs on my hands or my first time being arrested. My first incident happened with my mum, I remember it like it was yesterday. I had slept in after a long day at school, and I overslept past the time I was supposed to get up and open the door for my mum to get in. My sisters weren't home that night, and I slept so soundly I didn't hear her banging on the door or calling my name.

I don't know how she finally got into the house, but when she did, instead of gently waking me up as she could see it was an accident, she decided to wake me up harshly. She used what we called 'omorogun' in Yoruba (one of the three main languages in Nigeria) to hit me on my head.

Omorogun is a wooden stick used for cooking or stirring and creating foods like mashed potatoes. After the wooden stick hit my head I remember jumping up, feeling the heat rush to my head, and receiving a massive slap to my face in addition. I screamed for her to stop and she continued to beat me, grabbing the stick up off the floor. I was going crazy trying to understand why my mother would use a thick wooden stick to hit me just because I didn't open the door as I had fallen asleep on the couch.

I believe that was the first time I ever defended myself, I pushed her off me and screamed for her to stop. Instead, she instead reached over and grabbed onto my bra forcefully, trying to rip it. I refused to be humiliated and was struggling to push her off me when she went even further and bit my breast!

Yes, my mum started to bite my breast. She bit and fought me like I was her peer fighting over a man; it was sad. As she bit me and tightened her teeth on my skin, the pain got so extreme that I couldn't help but to hit her with my hands, slapping and struggling to get away from her. I was dragging myself along the floor, screaming for someone to help, when she grabbed my foot and viciously bit my toenail off.

    After it was all over, she took me to the hospital and paid for every medication I needed. While I was there I got calls from all my aunts and uncles and every elder that I knew telling me I had been in the wrong, and was as usual disrespectful. In most African cultures, the child was always wrong and the parents were always right, it's the way things were so as kids we had to just accept the scolding from the elders accessing the situation.

    I even got calls from the Mainhouse Faithful Ministries parish church praying for me. The prayer points they focused on were the devilish spirit of stubbornness in me, the spirit of anger, and the spirit of hatred against my mother. Not once did anyone listen address the fact that I was hit by a wooden stick, my breast was bitten, my toenail was bitten off, and I was the one laying in the hospital. But that was only the appetizer on the menu of punishment that my mother had planned for me. It seemed she didn't know how to separate being a mother and being a police officer. She picked me up from the hospital, put cuffs on my hands straight from the hospital bed, took me straight to the police station and locked me up for two days. That day always stuck in my soul, it felt like shattered glass in my heart every time I thought about it. They say children never forget, and I never forgot all the discipline I received. It manifests as scars on my body, each with a story attached.

      Suddenly I snapped out of thinking about my first arrest, I had hit my head on the police car when they were getting me into the back seat. I started to shed tears looking at Sandra play the false victim so perfectly. I told the police officer my story as he was collecting my info. He seemed somewhat nice and told me, "Family can at times be your destruction if you're not careful, I don't know what happened, but there's nothing I can do, I'm just following orders. If everything is resolved I advise you to keep your distance and love your family from afar."

Chapter 15

I never really knew how close the police department was until they drove me there that night. I was assisted out of the car with my hands behind back and the cuffs so tight on my hands. My robe was about to pop open, and it was only by God's grace that it stayed in place or I would have given them a free show. I felt like I was a part of a Halloween show or a stripper routine, because I didn't understand why they didn't let me dress properly.

They walked me up the stairs and straight to the front desk where the female police officer took out everything inside my pocket and placed it into a little envelope with my name on it. From there I was taken upstairs and into a room with computers, a mini-cell and other electronic devices with assigned police officers standing beside each piece of equipment. I was asked to remove any metal, shoelaces, belts, and anything else that seemed like a sharp object or a string while smartly replying to the officer: "I thought they took everything out of my pockets downstairs, and you can clearly see I'm only wearing a robe."

He said it was just protocol to tell me to remove anything they may have not seen downstairs. The female officer walked forward and said, "I can see you have shorts and a tank top on under the robe, so we will still take the belt from the robe away, we would hate to see you harm yourself with it."

She took the belt, leaving my chest far more exposed now that the robe was open. The tank she claimed I was wearing was a soft, see-through fabric, and I wasn't comfortable because I wasn't wearing a bra. I voiced this to her, but she seemed to not care. They went even further and walked me through a full body scan machine, like the ones at the airport, to see if they could find anything else on me.

Once the scanning process was completed I moved over to give more information to the police officer who was sitting down. While he filled in this information on his computer I was asked to stand by a blank wall where they took my mug shot. Once they took my mug shot I started to realize that Sandra must have cooked up a good story to tell them just to make me suffer.

The papers were being completed and I saw the words "Possession of Weapon" across the top. In shock, I questioned the officer, but he told me he was just filling out the paperwork, and there was nothing he could do.

After a few minutes I was taken back downstairs in handcuffs, when right in the hallway we stopped. Suddenly the office started to say, "You have the right to remain silent. Anything you say can and will be used against you in a court of law." He sounded like a robot as he said this to me, then he finally asked me what had happened, and I told him. He asked, "So where did you put the knife?"

I was shocked, my jaw dropped, and I replied "What knife?" He responded that my sister Sandra had told them I used a kitchen knife to threaten her and the kids, and that I hid the knife in my bags when the cops arrived. I told him she was lying and then I said he should look for the supposed knife in my bag and if he found it he should do a fingerprint test on it. He asked if I was confident that if they did a fingerprint I would be clear, and I cried "YES!" loudly. I even asked if they would lock Sandra up for the humiliation and lies against me if they saw her fingerprints on it. He replied only that he would let me know when the results were back, and that it may take 1 - 2 weeks.

    After this he took me into the prison cells which looked extremely dirty. First we had to walk past all the hallways filled with inmates. There were about 12 cells, and all were full except for one. The walls were filthy brown, the floors looked like they had peed frequently on them, and it looked like it had never been swept since the prison cell was constructed.
The specific cell he put me in was little, I mean very little, and the toilet smelled horrible. The little bench was near the toilet which was very uncomfortable. There was all sorts of writing on the wall, I'm guessing signatures of people who had passed through this

particular cell. Within an hour, a rough looking lady with tattoos who seemed like a hard- core lesbian was put in my cell with me. She said nothing, just walked back and forth and leaned on the wall all throughout the night. All night I tossed and turned on the little bench near the toilet, while keeping one eye open in fear that my cellmate might strangle me to death. She kept twisting her hair into mini dreads every time I looked in her direction.

I woke up at 8am, turning over in pain from sleeping on the wooden bench with my legs hanging off. The first thing I saw was my cellmate sitting butt naked on the toilet taking a poop. What a disgusting view to see so early in the morning. Another cellmate came to join us and it turned into a reunion between the previous cellmate, the new one, and one in the next block. They all talked loudly, and from what I could hear they had been here last week for the same thing: "jumping" (ganging up on someone and beating that person up).

The new cellmate who came that morning

was extremely disgusting. As she talked she kept spitting on the floor. Finally, we got some food: they brought us bagels with a single ham slice and no mustard or mayonnaise, just a plain bagel with ham and a juice box. We were all waiting for buses that would transport us to the courthouse where the judge would decide our fate.

The woman in Cell Seven kept on talking loudly, screaming and screaming to be released, she was making the others extremely angry. They kept telling her to shut up, but she only replied by cursing them out and laughing, she was having fun being a nuisance in the cell. One of the inmates said, "You fucking making noise and shit and fucking with niggas, I bet you don't even know who was arrested for murder, you gonna get your ass fucked up, just keep talking shit." After that statement it seemed to gradually get quieter.

Finally, the last bus came around 2:30pm and they were ready to load us up to go to the courthouse. Before we left the police department they attached twelve of us to a long chain that connected all of us together. It was like a long train with all of us - that way no one could escape. We all walked slowly towards the bus and headed towards the courthouse. We had no seat belts on so I figured if there was an accident someone would definitely be dying.

We got out at the court house and were told that if we were released our envelopes with our belongings would be at the entrance of the courthouse. We were all put in a cell, and then we were transported again to another cell. There was little doubt in between that the judge was angry and may not see any of us, it was possible we would all sleep another night in the cell. We heard that a fight broke out in the courthouse and that's what caused the delay, Then and there I prayed to the Lord to save me from this mess and reveal the truth concerning my situation.

Eventually things started to move along, and we were assigned to lawyers provided by the government. My assigned lawyer kept our conversation very brief and told me I was going to be released, that my sister had come forward the same night they cuffed me to tell them that she had been angry and only said whatever came to her head at the moment.

In the courtroom they were very serious, just like in the movies: no phones, no talking, and you had to be respectful and stand up as the judge walked in. I waited for a long time before my turn came, and many people had been arrested for resisting arrest, being under the influence of drugs, having weed, credit card fraud, trespassing, and one was even put on $75,000 bail - she was going to be transported to the main prison.

There was one lady who was arrested for breaking her boyfriend's windshield after he beat her up in front of her child for refusing to give him money for drinks. It's just crazy that some people like myself weren't meant to be there at all and had been arrested wrongfully. When it came to my turn, it went by quickly - I simply put my hands behind my back and nodded my head as the judge asked questions of my lawyer. Within a few minutes my case was tossed out.

Chapter 16

I was finally out, and I could smell the fresh air. After collecting my belongings in the envelope, I started to make my way back to Sandra's house with no idea of where else to head. I must tell you it was the most embarrassing long walk I have ever had in my life - I was walking in broad daylight in just my robe and no slippers. If it was Halloween I would have had an excuse for my look, but it wasn't even close to that time of year and if I was in the suburbs it wouldn't have been as embarrassing as crossing the city streets looking like a mentally challenged lady on crack. Cars drove by slowing down to get a good look and a good laugh. I stood by a bench at the CTA station reflecting on how I had come to be there. I sat there for hours with the few of my belongings I was able to recover from Sandra's house. The CTA station I sat at was next to her house at Bryn Marr Red Line, and people looked at me funny as they swiped their metro cards to get on the train.

Whenever I saw someone from Sandra's neighborhood I would bow my head down as if I was asleep to avoid embarrassment and questions. After a while the CTA lady noticed me and asked if I was okay. It's truly a great thing to say a simple "Hi" to a stranger. I remember going through this train station before and greeting her before swiping my card. I believe that's how she recognized me and came up to ask if I was okay. I told her what happened, and she felt so bad for me that she bought me lunch as she was clocking out for the next person to come take their shift.

    As soon as the CTA lady walked away and said goodbye I started to eat like I had been starving for years and years. I have never eaten a whole sandwich that fast in my whole life. I felt full and gradually started to shut my eyes when just then I heard a voice calling my name. I thought I was hallucinating as I heard it over and over. I sat up and looked around to see who was calling and it was a friend from a while back that I met at the church. She was from

Nigeria as well. I hadn't seen her much because I had been trying to avoid anyone and everyone as I hurt silently in Sandra's house looking for a job and trying to start my life. I stood up and ran straight to her, hugging her like she was the last person on Earth. As we pulled back from hugging each other, tears flowed down my eyes.

Pelumi: "Why are you crying? Please stop!"

Me: "I have been through a lot since I last saw you."

Pelumi: "I'm sorry, I just left your sister's house, and she told me you moved out."

Me: "She threw me out with all my things."

Pelumi: "Are you serious? She looked very calm when I asked after you."

Me: "She is a liar and a pretender, just like the fool she is with."

Pelumi: "This is just crazy, because I am facing the same thing."

Me: "What happened to you?"

Pelumi: "Hmmm . . . you don't even want to know, let's sit down."

Me: " okay so, tell me what happened."

Pelumi: "I have been chased out of my place."

Me: "Your family threw you out?"

Pelumi: "No, my roommate couldn't afford the rent and was moving. So, I can't stay there when the landlord comes. So, I'm homeless now."

Me: "Wow are serious? Pele, I'm sorry."

Pelumi: "Your case is even worse because you have a sister here and couldn't even depend on her."

Me: "Where is your family?"

Pelumi: "I was able to call them, and they want to send money to me to come to Maryland where my aunty is. I am still waiting for the money. I didn't tell them I am homeless yet. I don't want my mum to panic and have hypertension."

Me: "But why don't you tell them, so they won't wait and can send the money quickly?"

Pelumi: "I will survive for a couple of days, don't worry."

Me: "No! No! No!"

Pelumi: "Funke please stop, we need to focus on where we will sleep for tonight."

Me: "I have asked around for the shelters in the area, but they are closed for renovation, there was a fire outbreak just recently. We can't even make the other ones, the cut-off time to line up has passed. They won't even allow me enter with these bags."

Pelumi: "Let me help, help you with this bag right here."

Me: "Thank you my friend."

Pelumi: "You know what, I have a plan, we can ride the train back and forth."

Me: " Is it safe?"

Pelumi: "We have no other option, because at the park they will send us out. The park closes by 11pm."

Me: "Oh, okay, why don't we take turns to sleep and watch over each other so no one harms us?"

Pelumi: "That's a plan, the red line should be safe, we will take the cart where the conductor is."

Me: "Alright, let's go."

Pelumi and I rode the red line back and forth throughout the whole night! There was only one time we had to get up - when a particular conductor wanted to park the train and went around to drive everyone off. It was super annoying to wake up, drag our bags, and run across the train platform to get on the other train heading back.

In the mornings we would wake up and head to the public centers to take a shower. After we freshened up we lined up at the food centers that gave food out to the homeless. We had list full of all the food pantries that gave out cooked food, and dined on hot chicken soup, turkey sandwiches, and crackers.

We would spend the rest of the day sitting on the computer at the library, and by evening we would be back on a bus to ride all throughout the night. We had even gone to an LGBTQ (Lesbian, Gay, Bisexual, Transsexual, and Questioning) center once. They gave us free food, metro cards, free clothes, and even took us to the movies. I guess all these things were designed to help us get off the streets and feel loved. I remember they also offered job search services and housing applications. We weren't lesbians but they still accepted us as their own.

  Unfortunately, Pelumi and I had a huge fight one night when I discovered that she had lost the bag I gave her to help me hold. I was so angry that after the argument I just walked away. I couldn't understand how she could lose my bag, and I didn't want to listen to her give excuses for losing it. I just jumped on the first bus I saw.

  After about twelve stops the bus driver said the next one would be his last stop. I got off the bus and walked into a dark street with very few lights on. Just as I turned around to ask the bus driver for directions to the nearest train station, he drove off. I roamed around waiting for another bus to drive by, and as I did I saw a guy standing by the corner smoking and watching me wander around in circles. I started to look in my pockets for the metro cards I had collected at the LGBT community center. Just as I pulled them out, the bus approaching me changed its header to "OUT OF SERVICE USE NEXT BUS." I got frustrated and started to head back towards where I left Pelumi. It wasn't until I was almost back to where she was that I looked back and noticed the man I had seen near the bus stop was walking behind me. I started to walk faster, and he called out to me asking if I was lost.

Man: "Hey - you lost?

Me: "No, don't worry."

Man: "Are you sure? Because I was waiting for the bus also."

Me: "Oh, you were?"

I slowed my walking to let him catch up.

Man: "Yeah, I was, those stupid buses - always late."

Me: "I am just gonna walk back to Halsted, it's not far I think."

Man: "Oh, I'm going to the same area, I know a short cut."

Me: "Oh okay"

Man: "Wait, you are walking the longer route."

Me: "I'm fine this way, thank you."

Man: "If you're scared I understand, but trust me I am a normal guy - no bullshit."

Me: "Umm . . ."

Man: "I'm just showing you the shorter route, plus this place is lively, people are around, you are safe."

Me: "Well, you're right I guess, okay then."

Man: "So where you from?"

Me: "I'm from Nigeria, and you?"

Man: "Nigeria? Oh - the rich country! Isn't that where Eddie Murphy did *Coming to America*?

Me: "I'm not sure, I haven't even seen the movie."

Man: "It's a great movie! Are you a princess in your country?"

Me: "I wish I was, I wouldn't be here right now if I was."

Man: "You are beautiful girl with a nice body."

Me: "Thank you."

Man: "Damn, you Africans always got thick bodies, like big soft asses."

Me: "Ummm . . . thank you sir."

Man: "Can I touch it a little . . . in the corner . . . right quick?"

Me: "I'm sorry, I don't do stuff like that."

Man: "I'm not asking for sex, just to feel on your big ass."

Me: "Sorry you can't, umm . . . I think I'll go back this way to find my way to Halsted."

We were in a dark alley behind Wrigley Field. The game had just ended, and it was so noisy. As I turned to walk towards where I could see a crowd, he pulled my bag. I started to get scared and told him, "Sir please, I don't want any problems, I am going to leave now."

He moved closer not saying a word, his eyes looked darker than normal as he forcefully grabbed my bag and tossed it to the side. It was my cue to run, but just as I tried to he grabbed me and pulled me in even closer.

I screamed as loud as I could, "HELP ME!" He head butted me with so much force I went blank and sort of dizzy and hit the ground. My eyes were blurry but I lifted my hands and started swinging in different directions to hit him and get him off me. I managed to hit him a few times even though I couldn't see clearly.

The next thing I felt was five heavy blows to my face, one right after the other, I felt like my nose was broken and my eyes were gone. I couldn't even open my mouth to scream my jaw was so damaged.

Suddenly, I felt the weight of his heavy body on top of me as he reached into my dress, pulling my underwear down to my knees with one hand while the other hand covered my face. With what little energy I still had I struggled to push him off, but he smacked my face again with such force that my neck felt like it snapped. I could feel tears rolling down my face and blood gushing from my mouth as he leaned in closer. He wickedly took access of my safe haven that only my future husband should have had the key to and brutally forced his manhood into my temple, breaking my walls of protection.

Hearing me scream, cry for help, and struggle for my last breath must have given him the satisfaction of his life. He leaned further, forcing his lips on mine and shoving his tongue into my mouth as I struggled to scream through the blood gushing out. I came close to passing out thinking I was probably going to die there.

When my head cleared and I came back to earth I bit down hard on his tongue, but once again he drew back and smacked me even harder while stabbing a sharp object straight into my breast. Still not satisfied he yanked my hair and turned me over aggressively pushing my face into the ground. I felt my mouth fill with the sand and rocks as he pushed himself further inside me.

He shoved his abomination, his wickedness into my last hope and took a reckless drive tearing my soul and womanhood apart. Not content with the emotional devastation of raping me, he completed my utter humiliation by standing up and ejaculating and urinating all over me. As he zipped up his pants he called me every name in the book then kicked and spat on me before he finally walked away. I listened to his footsteps fade away until it grew silent. I rolled over and tossed from side- to-side humming and groaning in pain until my body just shut down.

Chapter 17

I woke up in the hospital and looked to the side where I saw Pelumi sitting beside me. I screamed from the pain and began to cry as the rush of memories washed over me. The nurses walked in and tried to calm me down, but I just kept screaming, "I am finished, my life is over!"

I wanted to die. All my life I had seen rape on television and heard about it from people around me, but I never thought I would be one of the victims. After I had cried a bit I got weaker and blanked out again. The next time I woke up calmer, I had begun to accept my horrible fate. I knew I couldn't do anything to change my situation and I was tired of crying out to the heavens. I had a fight with Pelumi and I know she left the hospital. I sort of blamed her for what had happened to me. I wasn't sure if she returned while I was sleeping, but once I was discharged I couldn't wait for her.

Coming out of the hospital, I had no idea of where to go. I was used to doing the homeless routine with Pelumi, not on my own and I had no metro cards on me. I walked over to the bus stop and just sat there for a few hours. Suddenly a taxi slowed down and as I looked over into the car it was Mark!

Mark told me he went by the hospital to look for me after he had gotten the information from the nurses that I was raped. He told me they saw his business card in one of my pockets. I had forgotten that when I was waiting in his car after Sandra threw me out I had reached over to grab a business card from his dashboard.

Mark helped put my mind at ease when he said I could come stay with him for the time being, but I worried about going to stay with a man I didn't know. In the end the question was moot, after all I knew no one and had nowhere else to go. I hadn't really made many friends since I came to the US and I never heard from Pelumi again. My sister treated me like babysitter turned slave who stayed stationed in a cave of darkness and never saw the sunlight which i didn't give me much of a chance to go out and make friends.

Mark was kind enough to lend me his phone so I could call my mother back in Nigeria and let her know what had happened, but I regretted it as soon as she answered. My mum seemed to be more concerned about what I had said to my sister and barely listened when I said I had been locked up and spent the night in jail.

I didn't even bother to tell her about my rape because it would only hurt to hear her telling me to hush up about such silly accusations. She even told me to go back and beg my sister for a second chance, because she was the only one we had left in the family with an education and ability to financially support us.

I thought to myself "To hell with this," and I told my mother she could continue to kiss Sandra's ass for the money, but I wouldn't allow myself to be any further mentally damaged. I hung up the phone as she was calling: "Shut up! Stupid girl! Wouldn't you rather suffer and know you have someone securing you with money, so you are stable?"

Living with Mark was both uncomfortable and amazing at the same time. He stayed in a one bedroom on the north side of Chicago on Ridge Blvd. I say it was uncomfortable only because he gave up his one room just so I, a stranger, could enjoy the privacy and comfort. Mark moved into the living room and slept on the couch. He didn't even ask me to pay rent or electricity or gas bills while I stayed there. During the day I used his desktop computer to look for a job and start my school process.

At night, when he came back from work, he would ask nicely about how my school processing was going and the job applications I had filled out without it seeming like he was in my business. He was so polite that he would even check with me if a visitor was coming over to make sure it was okay. In return I made sure the house was clean and I cookedmeals for both of us, although I think my cooking skills may have needed help because whenever he bit into the meat he would make a funny face and I would bow my head down in shame.

Mark was hardly home, he mostly was out driving his taxi to make ends meet and to be able to send money back to his family to help support them. Although he was religious, he never forced Christianity down my throat, even though I shared the same beliefs with him. On Sundays I didn't have to attend church if I didn't want to. Mark was a single man and it seemed like most of his friends and fellow church members were always trying to link him up with a woman.

I could only imagine what the church members had to say about me living with him! They always had questions every time I saw them - questions like how we met, what kind of job did I have, how many bedrooms were in the apartment, all just to see if we were together.

I remember when Mark's little niece visited unexpectedly, he had offered to take her for a few days as her mother had an emergency and had to drive down to Washington D.C. Mark asked if I had anything to do that weekend and I said no-that I could help look after the girl while he was driving the taxi. I had forgotten I had signed up for a temporary gig at the National Museum. It was about 7am when I remebered and he had already gone to work: I couldn't miss out on the money, but I also didn't want to disappoint him on the one thing he asked me to do. So, I got the girl dressed and took her to work that day. I intentionally came in through the front door instead of the back to link her up with some of the other kids visiting the museum. The plan was to have her mix in with the high school students that were her age and height. She blended in perfectly and no one suspected, not even the school instructors guiding them. She toured the exhibitions for free with the school group, and whenever they were counting heads she would walk to the side like she was looking at something and then rejoined the kids when they were walking into the King Tut exhibit. She was a smart one and made the plan go smoothly.

When I took my break, I grabbed her to come eat some lunch as well. For the remainder of the day she just wandered around looking at the free exhibits. It was extremely risky, however, we made it through that day. I didn't tell Mark what happened that day and neither did she, just as I had instructed. Later he gave me a new and very pretty diary with some money inside to show his appreciation for staying with her that day. He had watched me over the past weeks sitting on the kitchen counter, facing the windows, just writing my sorrow in my diary as a way to remain sane. He knew just what it meant to me. The money went into my savings, and I smiled as I went to the bank thinking of how my own sister rarely showed her appreciation, instead she made it seem like it was my job to do.

Chapter 18

School started soon after that and I enrolled in a school in downtown Chicago where I was going to study banking and finance. Financial aid was covering most of the parts of schooling that I couldn't afford. When I needed a co-signer to complete the application, Mark made himself available. It's truly amazing how an outsider can be of more value to you than your family, even though they say blood is thicker than water. Through my school I started working as a teller for the MACH Bank in downtown Chicago, and I was determined to move up the ladder.

Handling cash really scared me because I hated being responsible for anyone's money. I believe that's why I never helped to keep anyone's money when I was young either. I wasn't afraid that I might steal it or spend it, but more that I would misplace their money. However I did a fantastic job at what I did. I understood what it meant to serve the customer and meet their needs. Lord knows I hated dealing with angry customers who would make scenes at the bank. I remember working extra hours and feeling so very tired at work.

Most days were demanding with long queues, especially during lunch hours when people were in rush. At the branch we tried our best to eliminate the long lines before the customers started complaining and got angry. The only lines we couldn't really control were the lines for other services where they needed a sit-down transaction other than depositing and receiving money.

The sit-down area or lines were for services like getting a document notarized, which mostly the manager had to do herself or himself. Some more services like banking verification documents for housing which tellers couldn't help out with except for the managers or the clerks with their own desk.

We were given daily and weekly goals, the tellers had to get sales which were the credit cards. We had to open credit cards to make our goals in the branch, usually after every transaction whether it's a deposit transaction or a withdrawal transaction the screen shows the type of questions to ask the customer like mortgage related questions or loans and more. Working at the branch as a teller I didn't have to follow the customer banking rules like you must deposit at least 500 dollars every month or pay a service fee, there weren't any minimum balance requirements needed either. On my way back home, I would sleep off missing my stop on the train then jumping out to take the next train back home. I usually took the red line train to work and back from work it wasn't easy but it's what I had to do.

    I had been living with Mark for a little over a year when he randomly asked if I had been speaking with my mum, and when I said no he persuaded me to call her. I remember he told me that if I didn't call my mother and resolve things with her that he would ask me to leave. So, I called her, but nothing had changed - after a few days she was already asking me to refund the ticket money that had brought me to the United States.

I actually wanted to gather all the money to pay her, so she would stop bothering me, but then I stopped myself and thought it was her duty as a mother to cover these expenses for her kids until they become productive members of society with great jobs. So, I ignored her calls until she got the message that paying her back for the ticket money was not gonna happen at all.

Chapter 19

A couple of weeks later my mother came with my aunt to visit Chicago. I only found out when I received a random phone call from her with a Chicago area code. My mother announced to me that Sandra was pregnant, and I wasn't surprised - to me she was like a baby making machine. I knew Sandra's tactics, I was pretty sure she was ready for my mother to help out with the kids.

In the African cultures it was typical that a grandmother would be available to take care of her grandchildren while her daughter went to work or got some rest. I wasn't sure about the American culture, but I guess hiring a nanny is usually what they do. I sometimes wondered if Sandra ever got any rest. She worked her ass off and paid all of the rent while her husband did shady businesses and dressed very well in his designer clothing.

According to my mum Sandra had told her I was living with a boyfriend, which she found out through people she knew at her church. My mother wanted to meet me on the coming Sunday, in two days. I met her at Sandra's church towards the end of the service. I was standing right in front of my mother and my aunt talking and catching up when Sandra walked over and gave them a mean look that said: "Oh - she is still alive?" My aunt and mother scolded me in front my sister for not greeting her properly, despite what she had done to me.

I did as they requested but I had already planted the seeds of hatred towards Sandra. It was too late to mend the gap between the two of us. Sandra proved me right: as they were about to go home my mum asked me to jump in the car with them as they were heading to the mall. Sandra told our mum that if I wanted to follow them to the mall I would have to take the bus and meet them there because there wasn't space in the car. My mother tried to force me into the car despite what Sandra said, but I didn't want to be insulted so I decided to go home.

When I left them, they were all in a good place, however a week later things had changed. My mum called me from another Chicago area code and told me she was heading to Maryland to stay with her friends and that my aunt was following her. While she was telling me this she was crying, and when I questioned her she told me she had to go and would call me back.

I called her multiple times during my shift at work and got no reply. I was so worried that I told Mark about it, and he told me to give her a day and pray for her that night. I guess the prayers worked because she called me very early the next morning to tell me what happened. Apparently, Sandra had asked her to babysit one day while she ran a quick errand. My mother said she refused and even complained that since she had been in America Sandra hadn't taken her out or bought anything for her, all she was doing was babysitting and not even getting a thank you for that.

Sandra got mad and said that if she couldn't help her there was no use for her to stay in her house anymore, that she would just go pay the nearby daycare to take care of the kids. My mother said she thought Sandra was just bluffing until she flung her things out along with my aunt's belongings. Sandra even called the police on her just like she did to me.

Sandra and her husband even went so far as to push them down the steps. I could have said I told you so, but at the same time it was sad that she had to see the kind of person her daughter had become. Sandra had become ruthless and cold and I didn't want our mother to see her this way.

Chapter 20

The following Monday, as I was getting dressed for work, I spent the whole hour debating calling in sick. It had been a long week, and I had so many assignments and research projects to complete for school, not to mention finding time to meet with my lecturer to assist me with citations. I needed the money though, so I didn't call off and got to work around 9am. That day the manager seemed to be in a bad mood - he told us we hadn't been bringing in enough new customers to open up checking accounts. I immediately made a note in my little pad to keep track of how many customers I was able to sign up that day. By lunchtime I was in a pretty good place, and at 12:30 I was in the backroom observing my 15 minute break: chatting with a co-worker about the Grammys and the performances at the award show.

Just as we were about to discuss the new music videos they had showed, my supervisor walked in to tell me there was someone asking for me in the waiting area. I seriously had no idea who it might be because I had never told anyone where my job was located, not even Mark. The more I thought about it as I packed up my snack, I figured it must be a customer who I had helped before that preferred to have me help them again.

As I opened the door into the banking area, I looked around and saw a couple of people waiting in the lobby. I looked over at my supervisor and he pointed in the direction of the person waiting for me, to my surprise it was Sandra. As I walked slowly over to her I wondered if she was bringing bad news, maybe that something had happened to our mum. My heart started to beat rapidly as I approached her, so as soon as I reached her I said:

Me: "Good afternoon. Please tell me everything is right with mum!"

Sandra: "What is good about the afternoon you fool?"

Me: "I am just greeting you, is everything okay?"

Sandra: "Everything will be okay when you and your stupid mum leave me alone!"

Me: "Sandra please, what happened this time?"

Sandra: "Well, your stupid mother is going around telling people how I mistreated her and disgraced her."

Me: "Well she told me you threw her out with our aunty."

Sandra: "Is that what she told you? And if I did, so what? Did she help me buy my house or help me pay the bills?"

Me: "But how can you throw your own mother out of the house?"

Sandra: "You clearly don't even know what happened, you were born a fool and always have been a fool! Do you really think I threw her out?"

Me: "I am far from a fool, and I believe her. After all, you threw me out and called the police on me. So, I actually believe it."

Sandra: "In your case you deserved it. You are a bastard child like your mother calls you every time, and a bastard child doesn't deserve a shelter. You are fuck-

-ing lazy and wanted to seduce my husband and ruin my marriage."

Me: "Why did you even decide to come to my job to talk about this rubbish. The last time I checked you weren't legally married and it's not my fault your husband keeps looking at me like a savage dog thirsty for a treat. He is not my type and it seems he is tired of you because you look like a linebacker playing for a football team! Oh, and this house you go around talking about, let it be clear you are renting! Stop giving yourself a higher platform than you actually deserve!"

Sandra: "OH!!! So, you have grown wings to reply me with insults now? You are now a big girl right?"

Me: "Yes, I learnt from the best, isn't that what you did all your life - terrorizing our mother for your pathetic father who didn't want to claim you as his child?"

Sandra: "You talk of fathers when yours hardly ever showed his face, ashamed of you and your sister. He could have saved his nutrients for a better set of children elsewhere than producing fools for kids."

Just as I was about to fire back, my manager walked over and told me to remember I was off break and needed to go back to my position and help the customers. I nodded my head just so he could leave, and

I could continue to attend to the fool who I regret calling my older sister.

Sandra: "Now before I leave I should let you know that you and your mother should never call me again for anything in your lives! If you are dying please find someone who cares to know, don't even dare dialing my number. When your mother dies you should bury her alone, and I really hope this stupid job can help with the funeral fees."

Me: "Sandra, God will punish you beyond imagination, you will suffer for the words you just said. I feel sorry your children having a very wicked person like you as a mother. Your credit card scamming, cocaine using husband will soon leave you for another woman."

Before I could finish getting the words out, Sandra slapped me across my face with all her strength. The customers looked around - shocked, the ladies sitting behind us stood up and headed out the doors. My Manager was walking towards us, but before he could get anywhere close I reacted in anger and slapped her right back.

I must have forgotten where I was and definitely had forgotten we were in the United States, where police officers could be here in a second to escort both of us out the doors. Sandra retaliated by beating on me with her bag, and I grabbed onto her, just swinging my hands across her face. I wasn't even sure if I was slapping or punching or scratching, I just knew my mission was to target her face and do damage. I wanted to leave a mark for her to remember whenever she got in front of the mirror.

My manger started screaming, "Stop this! This is a place of business, stop this!!" I overheard a customer saying, "Someone call the cops," and before I knew it we both were on the floor rolling back and forth, beating on each other brutally. She pulled on my hair and I also pulled on hers. I felt a sharp tremendous pain as Sandra pulled my earrings, ripping them off my ears as blood dripped down my crisp clean white shirt.

She climbed on top of me, grabbing my shirt and pulling apart the buttons, she pulled my bra to stretch it, she beat me with all her strength as I stared to feel myself giving up. I was screaming for help and the people around us start to pull her off me. As they separated us, I got a clear glance of myself - I had to hold onto my shirt to keep from exposing myself, and my arms were covered with blood stains and bite marks. It happened so fast that I honestly didn't even remember her biting me at all. The managers helped me up and into the back room. The customers and my fellow coworkers all looked shocked, whispering to themselves and looking so sorry for me, it was a huge scene that day. In the back room I was seated on the coach to relax.

Finally, my manager said: "What in the world just happened out there?"

I just kept on crying and saying "Why me?"

The manager said again, "Funke, who is that lady?"

I replied, "She is my sister, she came to embarrass me at work, she is just heartless."

Manager: "This is a place of work, why would you both bring this to the company?"

Me: "I didn't! She came here to find me. I have never told her where I work."

A coworker came in the back room saying, "We called the cops but the lady in the fight with Funke just left."

Manager: "Oh my God, this is a mess. The regional managers are going to make me answer to all this."

Me: "I'm really sorry, I'm really sorry. I didn't mean for things to happen like this. I should have just called the police immediately when I saw her, I should have known."

Manager: "I think you should just close out your computer, in fact never mind, I'll close it out for you. Just go home, rest, and figure out this personal problem."

Me: "Please, I don't want to lose my job, please, I've been good and been doing my work well, please."

Manager: "Funke, please get off the floor, I didn't say you are losing your job. You need to go home - your clothes are torn and covered with blood stains. Please go home and get rest."

Me: " okay, I'm sorry again for bringing this branch such shame, I'm really sorry."

Manager: "Please just go home and rest, I will call you before we close out for the day."

As I got myself together like the manger had asked I felt extremely embarrassed. I noticed coworkers coming to use the bathroom back-to-back so they could catch a glimpse of me looking terrible. As I walked past them I felt so terrible that I couldn't even look up, I just kept my head lowered and facing the ground. When I opened the door to the main lobby I saw the same customers standing in the lobby, waiting to see the conclusion of what had happened to me. I felt like I was taking a walk of shame as my manager escorted me to the door. As I walked between the customers I could hear them whispering things like: "That's her," "OMG, she looks terrible," "Is that blood on her shirt?" and, "Did they just fire her?". My fellow tellers all followed me to the door with their eyes. I had to take a cab home, I couldn't stand the thought of people staring at me all through an entire train ride.

Mark wasn't home when I reached the house, and I was glad so he wasn't. I didn't want him to hear about the shameful fight I had engaged in at work, or that my own sister wanted to ruin me. I took off every piece of my clothing and threw them all in the garbage, I didn't want any reminders of today. I put some peroxide and an ointment cream on my ear before adding a bandage to cover it up. My vision started to blur as I stared into the mirror, I heard a text message come in, it was from Sandra. I wanted to delete it immediately. I was so angry I was burning with ideas for revenge, but most of all I was hurt. So, I opened the text.

Message from Sandra:
You are beyond stupid! Your foolish father was a mistake upon our mother's life, abortion should have been her first thought. You are a bastard, a prostitute, a whore! Used product. You are useless, nothing you will ever do will turn out good. You are lucky we are not in Nigeria, I would have had the area boys deal

with you: rape you and, beat you mercilessly until you fell down and died! People like you are not needed on this Earth, you are a waste of space. Dumb bitch, daft representation of your foolish father, I regret being associated with you! Your mother can continue to support you. She herself needs help. Well done, you have finally gotten her to fight for you. If you people continue talking about me, may you not have peace in the whole of Lagos! Worthless piece of shit, you should have joined your sister to die. Ever since you fools joined the family, I knew it was going to be trouble. Wicked soul and heartless fucking bitch, hurry up and die so I can rejoice at your funeral and spit on your grave! Don't ever call or text this number or I will call the police on you again.

After I read the message I started typing faster than I ever had before in my life. But about two paragraphs in I stopped myself, thinking: "Why should I stoop so low as to engage in this foolishness?" What I had originally written was: "You are a fool and I can't even begin to comprehend the level of foolishness you have reached, but I think you should forget me as your sister and don't bother talking to me until you die." I cleared the text message and decided to be the bigger person like I have been told so many times in my life. It was clear from the text how much hatred she had within her, and it was getting to the point where I suspected if she ever had me in a quiet place with my back towards her she would stab me without even giving it a thought. Sandra hated me, and anyone who read that text would never believe we shared the same mother.

My manager, who had assured me that he would call by the end of the day, never called. The next morning, when I called to see what was going on and when I was scheduled to work next, he was not available. Later they told me he was on his lunch break. Later again he was on the phone but would call me back. I had to wait a whole other day before he finally called me back and told me the branch had decided to let me go. I had, "exhibited an unprofessional behavior that could have endangered the customers." He went on to say that the episode had contributed to their low credit card sign ups and transactions for the day since so many customers had exited the branch during the busy hours. I pleaded, cried, sobbed, and begged until he said, "This is the decision of the upper management, they have assessed the situation and reviewed the footage from that day. If it were left to me I would have forgiven you and moved on. I know your work ethic is tremendous, but I'm sorry, there is nothing I can do at this point." He didn't need to say anything else, the message had finally sunk in.

    I felt pain, like my world had stopped. Thinking of starting all over again to search for a job left me suicidal, depressed, frustrated, and just plain angry. I had nobody to talk to. If I called my mother, she would say: "Well I have my own problems, I can't really talk right now," so I just grabbed a pen and wrote like I always did. It felt like a release to put all of the negative energy into my pen and dump it onto a piece of paper to lock away my pain.

I wrote this piece and called it "Countdown to Death."

Countdown to Death

It was the worst thing ever to be under the same roof as a loved one, but to still have to look over your shoulder. It's quite normal to me, and it has become a ritual to sleep with one eye open. As I stand in the kitchen I smile, looking at the shelves just in case I may need to grab a knife. Our family portraits seem so perfect, but there is more to them than other people can know or see.

What does it matter anyway? If I was helpless on the side of a mountain, my sister would be all smiles and push me off the cliff. My mother would be too busy to even look over the cliff and call 911. If I was drowning, my sister would push my head further down in the water and my mother would be too busy counting her money. If a single dollar was missing she would say to me: "Well I have my own problems right now, I'll save you later." My life has been a painful-mess. Hell on Earth and torture in my dreams. Father Lord save my soul and give me just enough peace to remain sane.

Chapter 21

After a few days I realized I had to snap out of my depression and actually go find help. So, I researched a plan for how to go about job searching and getting government benefits. I started with food stamps, otherwise known as the Supplemental Nutrition Assistance Program or SNAP. SNAP helps people with limited income buy food. I remember searching for the address over the Internet and mapping the way there from my house. The website mentioned they would open at 8:30am, and I arrived at a time I felt was extremely early only to discover I probably was already number fifteen in line. The security guard opened the door at 8:30am sharp. Everyone picked a number and sat down to wait for their number to be called. The TV in the waiting area was kept either turned off or on but with the volume set super low, there were no magazines or anything else to keep ourselves busy while we waited. It was about 9:45

when my number was finally called, and the lady who took it asked for my Social Security card and state ID to enter into the system. I then had to take a seat and wait another hour for my name to be called again. A man finally took me over to a little cubicle in the corner and asked if I was working, paying any bills, who I was living with and a whole series of questions to determine if I would qualify for food stamps. When I told him I wasn't working, he asked if anyone was assisting me and I immediately answered yes. It was the first thing that came to my mind, little did I know he would ask me to bring back a letter from the person assisting me stating how much they were giving me. I didn't want Mark to know that I had applied for food stamps, I was afraid he would look at me differently, so I decided to forge a letter from the person supposedly assisting me.

In the letter I wrote:

To whom it may concern,

My name is Ralph Williams. I am a friend of Funke Adedayo. I assist her with money to buy food and move around in the city daily. I usually give her a hundred dollars to use. I am currently away in London for business, but you can email me at <u>LifeisFab346738@yahoo.com</u> with any questions.

Thank You,
Ralph Williams

    I took this letter to the Government Stamp Benefit Office the next day with high hopes that everything would go well. The man at the desk collected the letter and told me to wait five business days for a reply. I waited and nothing came in, so I went back to the office again. This time the worker told me I needed to provide proof that I was living at the address that I said I was.

    As I stood up, my face clearly showing the exhaustion of going back and forth, he told me he would go ahead and approve me for emergency food stamps. I was so happy and thankful, and even though he told me to bring in a proof of address document, once I got my benefit card I never went back. I was given $200 dollars per month to buy food and nothing else.

The first time I went to the grocery store with the benefit card I spent about $113 dollars on fruit, microwave pizza, hot wings, cookies, candy, ice cream, cereal, and juice. My cart was overflowing and the bags were almost too heavy to carry but I made it home. I remember taking my time arranging the fridge and the cabinet with the foods items smiling back at me. I kept opening the fridge over and over, hardly believing that I had so much food available to me. It was like I needed to pinch myself to wake up from a dream. For someone who just lost her job and had a huge blow out with her sister, it didn't show. I didn't lose weight at all, in fact I gained weight, the food stamps did that to me as I kept on eating and eating like there was no tomorrow.

During that particular school semester, I was taking a mandatory general literature class. We had to read three novels in order to pass: *Memoirs of a Geisha*, *One Flew Over the Cuckoo's Nest,* and *Wuthering Heights*. I only read *Memoirs of a Geisha* about halfway and then I got tired, so I purchased the audio version and listened to it when I was on the train coming and going to school. The audio version was word for word as the novel was written, and it was enough for me to pass the test. I hardly even opened the other two novels, the questions asked in relation to *One Flew Over the Cuckoo's Nest* I was able to answer from watching the movie. I passed that class with a C grade which was good enough for me. In the beginning I had a 4.0 GPA for most of my general classes. All of the students who received straights As in the four classes they took were sent a letter of congratulations from the school.

July 27, 2007
Funke Adedayo
1074 N. Retten Blvd
Chicago, IL 60688

Dear Funke,

Congratulations on being named to the President's List for the Spring 2007 Quarter! Your term GPA of 4 has qualified you for this unique distinction. You are a credit to the educational facility, yourself, and your family. Your outstanding academic work will be an asset to you in attaining your career goals.

Congratulations!

Sincerely,
Henry Williams
Vice Presidents of Academics

Chapter 22

It was around the next semester that I made a new profile on a social media site called FaceTools. I uploaded a random picture from a modeling company I had found online. It wasn't that I was ugly, but I worried that someone might recognize me. My height, weight, eye color, and hair color were all absolutely correct. I wrote about my hobbies, what kind of music I liked, and things like that, but none of it brought me someone sane enough to have a decent conversation with without talking about sex. It was a blog post that I uploaded in a group chat forum which attracted a certain guy named Marcus Steele. He messaged me to introduce himself and ask where I was from, and the moment I told him I was from Nigeria the conversation went to another level.

Marcus: "Wow, ur Nigerian !!!!!"

Funke: "Yes I am, why are you so excited?"

Marcus: "Because when I saw the name Funke in the group, I just knew you were Nigerian."

Funke: "LOL, yup yup."

Marcus: "What city do you stay in?"

Funke: "I stay in Chicago for now."

Marcus: "For now?"

Funke: "LOL, yea, feel like moving somewhere else."

Marcus: "Where?"

Funke: "Hmmm . . . New York, or Paris, just move there and start life fresh away from stuff. Anyway, where do you stay?"

Marcus: "I stay in Atlanta, Georgia, more specifically Athens, Georgia."

Funke: "I have never been to Atlanta, except for when I did a layover when coming to Chicago from Nigeria."

Marcus: "I mostly stay in Athens, the quiet part, kinda like a suburb and Atlanta is the city, the party place."

Funke: "How many minutes away is Athens from Atlanta?"

Marcus: "It's roughly about an hour and twenty minute drive."

Funke: "Oh okay, that's not too bad. So where are you from originally?"

Marcus: "Well, I was born in Atlanta, but my dad is African from Nigeria and my mum is white. So, I'm mixed."

Funke: "Oh wow!! So when last did you visit Nigeria?"

Marcus: "Wow, must have been ten years ago I think, I can't really remember."

Funke: "Oh geez! You need to visit soon, a lot of things have changed."

Marcus: "I keep hearing that from my family back there, but when Nigeria can have trains, smooth roads filled with traffic lights, and get rid of those barbaric yellow bus drivers then I'll be excited and motivated to visit, but for now I'm good."

Funke: "Lmaoooooo! I feel u on that lol, Naija is doing better tho real talk! They have come a long way. Can you speak Yoruba?"

Marcus: "Barely! I only hear Yoruba when my dad is mad at me and starts screaming in Yoruba."

Funke: "Lmaooo Naija Dads can be so annoying."

Marcus: "lol they are just amazing, aren't they?"

Funke: "Totally!!!"

    We chatted for about three hours that night. We would take breaks and then come back to chat through the social media platform. By the night's end we had exchanged numbers, and that's when he told me his name was Wale, and after that I didn't feel the need to logon to the chat room again. I was already enjoying his chat so much. Eventually we started talking over the phone, and for most of our conversations I was always giggling and blushing on the other end. Before I knew it, I started to get morning text messages saying, "Good morning sunshine, hope you slept well," and night time text messages saying, "Good night, Sweet dreams."

    Wale came into my life as a great distraction. At times we would be talking, and both fall asleep without hanging up, so we would hear each other snoring and that made it seem like we slept right beside each other. The culture similarity really sped things up, and eventually he asked about my family that I hardly spoke of. He was different, and I don't mean different like he spoke special words that made me melt and I wanted to marry him, and have his babies, and all that good stuff. He was different in the sense that he tried to relieve my stress when I had problems or complaints, like the time he shocked me towards the end of my semester. I was taking a class that had to do with product development.

  Wale offered to help me, and I took it as a joke at first until I started to get emails from him with dozens of articles to pick from to complete my project. The first email I opened said, "Baby, I know I said I would find 15 articles for you, but then I decided I would give you a couple FULL sites so you can search through them for multiple articles. You should be able to come up with WAY more than 15, lol. Hope it helps! I'll start looking for the pictures and send you some adverts." I read it and was so thankful for a sweet individual who really wanted to help me generally and be there for me.

Wale was a medicine student and that demanded a lot of his time, so the fact that he made time to help me out with my homework really meant a lot to me. For someone in another state who I hadn't even met yet, he really did instill happiness into my soul. I wanted to go further with him and see where it would go. The day for finals came, and I presented my work and got an A (with Wale's help of course), but with my finishing touches I scored the goal.

Chapter 23

Since meeting Wale, I was in a better state of mind, feeling happy to wake up every day and not feeling depressed or thinking I might die in my sleep. I got a job at a retail store which I called modern day slavery. I didn't like folding clothes and then having a customer come and mess up the pile five minutes later, all the while staring you in the eye. For the first month I was energetic, going above and beyond, running back and forth to get appropriate sizes for the customers, always willing to close the store when most of the associates didn't. I came to work on time and welcomed each and every customer through the door with a smile, but I must tell you, after a month, honestly I was over it.

The job started to get crazy and they started cutting our hours, I went from about 24 hours a week (even though I had been promised 40 hours in the beginning), to only four hours, sometimes eight if I was lucky. They kept saying there weren't enough hours because they weren't making enough sales, but they kept hiring more people, that's the part I didn't really understand.

    I knew they were in trouble when the employee discount went from 25% to 10%, and they changed their return policy to only offer store credit rather than cash back. I was tired of the company even though I was fairly new to it, and I started making my own rules - not that it was any good for the company, or myself for that matter. I took so many multiple breaks during my four hour shift in the fitting room -I would act like I was cleaning and taking clothes back to the sales floor, but instead I would find an empty fitting room towards the back and sleep in it. I would lay on the benches in the fitting room for 30 mins, and then take my assigned 15-minute break. Whenever a customer messed up my piles of t-shirts, I would just pick them all up and dump them in an empty fitting room for another coworker to fold.

    I have never really had friends up to that

point, but I did make friends at the store as Wale had suggested. These friends took me out to places I had never really expected to go, I remember my first time going to a fashion show they took me to. I volunteered just so I could get in for free and go backstage. I discovered fashion shows take a lot of work, and a lot of people are in involved, starting with the person who runs the production show, to the models, stage constructors, designers, and graphic designers.

During the actual show it was cool to finally get an answer to my question: "How do the models change so quickly back stage?" I learned that they have volunteers to remove their clothes and help them into the next outfit.

As soon as a model walked backstage, she would head straight to the people by the edge of the curtains and start taking her clothes off. While one person worked on her shoes, another two would be assigned to the upper body. If it was a dramatic outfit, she may have up to five people working on her shoes, dress, and accessories.

I had an embarrassing moment when a model stood in front of me and just dropped her clothes so she was standing naked. I stood frozen, staring at her perfectly crafted breasts, I was about to look even down further when she screamed "Um, what are you looking at? I'm going back out after her, please hurry up!" That woke me up out of my trance, and I started to replace her clothes for her to hit the runway.

The after party was held usually held in a large basement, and right in the middle was the dance floor. At each corner, and all along the wall people were flirting with each other, kissing, guys putting their hands up the model's skirts, and the models giggling as the hands went up their skirt and grabbed their butts. The parties were generally pretty wild for the most part.

As a general rule, one which I learned from the movies, I wouldn't take a drink from someone if I didn't see it being made in front of me. I also knew I should never walk away from my drink or turn my back on it, because it only took a few seconds for someone to slip in a pill. I'm sure that night I had a lot of guys mad at me because I refused to drink anything they brought my way. Everyone was having a great time despite all the drugs.

The party was going well until we heard a bunch of guys throwing stones at the window. I overheard a girl say that the guys wanted to come in, but no one knew them. In her words, they were just "thugs up the block trying to come get wasted and get some pussy."

The party host wanted to let them in, saying: "Hell, if they got some liquor, bitch, let them in, it's a bunch of niggas and niggarettes in in this motherfucker anyway, they will fit in perfectly." The girl replied, "Well, do what you wanna do, but me and my bitches 'bout to bounce when them thugs come up in here." The next thing we knew, the guys started to bang on the windows even louder, requesting to come in. A few guys had gone outside to confront them.

I was already thinking of leaving: I hated the smell of cigarettes - it stuck to my clothes and weave giving them a terrible smell. I couldn't find my coworkers -ers or the friends who had brought me to the party, so I decided to make my way out. I moved through the crowd and started to knock on the bathroom door but someone opened it. There was a boy and girl in there, his pants were all the way down and she was sitting on the toilet seat with her breast hanging all out of her bra with dollars bill sticking out from the bottom of it. The girl was the same model that had yelled at me at the show earlier.

For a quick second I thought to myself, "Wow, a model by day and a prostitute at night." His penis was extremely erect, and it didn't take a rocket scientist to know she was giving him a blow job in there. To add insult to injury he said, "Hey sexy, you wanna join us?" The girl interrupted, "It ain't that kind of party, and bitch what the fuck you looking at? Shut the door!" I slammed shut in disgust.

There were a pair of girls right outside the bathroom, gossiping so loudly that I'm sure everyone walking by could hear them.

Girl One: "Girrlllll, tell me why Shawn up in the bathroom with that model chick getting his dick sucked?"

Girl Two: "Bitch I don't care what she doing, all I know is I wanna see how big his dick is, I heard that shit like them African anacondas, big as a motherfucker."

Girl One: "I know that's right, I just wanna touch it though, I ain't doing too much with him."

Girl Two: "How you just gonna touch, you stupid for that. You need to touch it, spit on it, slap it, and sit on it and satisfy yourself. Girl get your life honey!"

I had never been around bold (or should I say desperate) girls who were craving a man's manhood like they were. It was shameful to see them acting like that. At that point, I decided I would hold my pee till I got home, and I was just leaving, when out of nowhere we heard a loud noise. Everyone started to look around, and the DJ turned down the music, and again we heard a loud sound, but this time it hap pened three times, one right after the other. Someone shouted, "Them thugs outside is shooting!" Just like that, everyone started to run towards the back door - it was like the end of the world. All the girls in heels were running like they were in the Olympics! Some of them fell on the steps and got stepped on from the people running behind them. People got pushed, hit with bottles, and it seemed like the thugs had a few of their members waiting at the backdoor. Our only escape options were to get beat up with hands and bottles at the backdoor or go through the front where the guys had guns and say goodbye to our lives.

    We all fought our way through the backdoor and ran towards the train station, following the one smart girl who took off her heels. It felt like if you stopped to take off your shoes you would get shot, so we just kept on running. On our way we saw a police officer driving around, and some of us screamed, "They're down the street," and kept on running. It was one of the scariest nights of my life. As we got to the train station, we ran up to the booth where the worker was and started mumbling, crying, and screaming. He came out and opened the gates for us to run onto the next approaching train. I don't think I ever took a Blue Line train again as they remind me of that horrible night.

When I finally got home, I got on my knees and thanked the Lord. I felt selfish because I hardly ever prayed except when I was asking the Lord to protect me, but at least I thanked him for saving my life that night. I didn't tell a soul about what had happened, and I stopped showing up to that job. They called and left messages that I was a "no call, no show," and then a week later they called for me to come and pick up my paycheck, but I never did.

Chapter 24

After a month or so I yearned to see some different scenery - to take my mind off of school, and not having a job. So, I decided to take a trip to finally meet Wale in Atlanta. I bought a round trip ticket for $270 on a student discount website, and I planned to stay with him for two weeks, I wasn't thinking of being smart, all I knew was that I was in love, and someone cared for me, and I was going to enjoy their company. I had never travelled within the US before, so I took my passport and then the ticket agents told me my regular ID was good enough. If there was one thing I learned in the airport, it was not to dress super cute, because you just end up removing all your accessories, shoes, and belts at the security points.

All through the plane ride I kept thinking of the risk I was taking to meet someone I barely knew and had met over the Internet. I told Mark I was traveling to see a friend from school, but didn't tell him the ex-

-act details, just that it was in Athens, Georgia in case I got murdered. On landing at the airport, I took my time looking for my luggage. As soon as I switched on my phone I got a text message from Wale saying he was running late in traffic, so I stayed towards the entrance doors looking cute, sitting on the benches guarding my luggage.

When I finally received a text from him saying he was parking, I started to adjust my clothes, checked my hair, and added some lip gloss to make sure I looked super cute the moment he laid eyes on me. I stood outside the entrance doors with my bags, and suddenly he was walking towards me. I recognized him immediately because we had skyped multiple times before I even bought the ticket to Atlanta so I could see how he really looked. He must have been a bit shy, as he gave me a quick hug and then helped with my luggage.

When we got to the parking lot he couldn't remember where he parked, and I giggled to myself that he must have been thrown off track by my stunning looks. We found his car parked at a little corner and I started to feel frightened that maybe it was a kidnap plot, and I was looking everywhere while he put my luggage in the boot.

As soon as he had put all my belongings in the boot, he stretched out his hand and hugged me properly for the first time. He reached over, looking into my eyes, and just as I was beginning to blush, he planted a kiss on my lips. Rather than enjoying the kiss, I started wondering if he was trying to have sex with me the first day, or just confirming I was attracted to him.

After our long kiss, we got in the car to drive to the downtown part of Atlanta. We got out of the car and he took me to a Body Museum exhibition down at 18th street. He had already purchased the tickets and had a dinner date set up. He was so sweet, even though he looked extremely nervous, but over all I really liked him so far. The exhibition gave us a chance to look into the systems of the human body (skeletal, muscular, nervous, respiratory, digestive, urinary, reproductive, endocrine, and circulatory). He kept apologizing and saying things like, "I'm sorry to have brought you to this lame kind of place for the first day," and all I responded was, "You know I can't really digest all this and enjoy it if you keep interrupting me with a million apologies all at once," and then I smiled, grabbed his hand, and walked further towards the second floor.

After the Body Exhibit we had dinner. I had never even had dinner outside in a fancy restaurant like that, much less been on a dinner date. I couldn't look directly into his eyes, especially being in the presence of others in a public place. The food was amazing, and so was the service. Wale thought the service was horrible and the food was just okay, but I gave it a grade A since I'd never really been out to eat at a restaurant, so what did I have to compare it to?

On finally reaching his place in Athens, I was so tired. We brought the luggage in, and right away he gave me a silly warning to beware of his talkative roommates, adding that the best way for me to avoid their long talks was to stay in his room. Well, fortnately, they weren't even home that night, so we settled down and talked all though the night. We cuddled eventually as we drifted off and didn't wake up until 1PM the next day.

Wale did all the cooking, he didn't let me cook anything. Well, to be honest, I didn't know how to cook, so I gladly stayed back and let him take charge of the kitchen, serving me the best of Atlanta's excellent food. We both enjoyed playing video games, which was weird, he didn't have to teach me, I had experience playing them back in Nigeria at my cousin's house. We would play video games all day and all night, taking breaks to grab a bite and then sitting back down to finish the mission. In fact, we played for two days straight and didn't even take a shower.

By the third day we went out to check the mall and see a movie, and ended up paying for one movie and sneaking in to three more movies after the first one. We broke all the rules of the movie theater, except for using our cell phones. During the movie Wale would randomly tell me how good looking I was and give me kisses. We, of course, smuggled in our own snacks, and he put his feet up on the chair in front of him to relax properly during the movie. We even enjoyed chilled beers we had brought in a tiny keep-cool case. We spent the whole day at the theaters and that night we drove to a faraway place.

On our way we stopped to grab some snacks at a gas station, kissing all throughout the store aisles. We parked the car and walked over a tiny bridge and into an open football field with half of the lights on. I was a little scared as I grabbed onto his hands and tightened my grip. He could tell I was afraid, and whispered in my ear, "I got you." We spread bedsheets and blankets on the grass right in the middle of the field. While he was prepping up the blankets and placing drinks and snacks out, I kept looking around in fear of wild animals or a killer on the loose, waiting to run out onto the field to attack us. I was so paranoid, but tried my best to not let it show as he had planned this wonderful night for us.

    We grabbed some food and talked about everything from music, to our careers, our families, and a hundred other things. We laid there staring at the stars, and it all came natural to just talk without awkward pauses. From the stars we suddenly started to talk about aliens, and he asked if I thought the field was a place they could possibly land and abduct us to their planet. I was fascinated by things like aliens and the Bermuda Triangle.

    Wale knew about all of it and updated me on most of the current findings. As he was talking about the Bermuda Triangle, he grabbed me closer to him and placed my head on his chest, covering our bodies with the blanket. Wale explained to me that the Bermuda Triangle wasn't just a myth, and we argued about that until I finally gave up, and he continued to talk, telling me about how the triangle is formed between Florida, Bermuda and Puerto Rico.

    He told me about how the planes that crossed over got sucked in as the water started to spin, and that the electronic signals of the planes got messed up and then they just vanished from the radar. He said that's why planes began to go around the Triangle, and never over it, to get to Puerto Rico, turning a three hour flight into a four hour one. The thought being sucked into a kind of vortex and coming out in another world frightened me, so I tried to get him to stop talking about it, but he continued like a geek.

    I didn't want to fight, so I continued listening. Wale said there were pyramids all over the world: one in Egypt called Djoser, one in Italy called Cestius, Uxmal Pyramid in Mexico. Chavin de Huantar in Peru, the Great Pyramid of Cholula in Mexico, Nubian pyramids at Meroe in Sudan, Ziggurat of Ur in Iraq, Tikal pyramids in Guatemala, a pyramid peeking out from the huge icebergs in Antarctica and even more he couldn't remember at the moment. He mentioned the Mayan calendar ending soon, and that it meant the world was ending, so the rich people were building underground bunkers.

    He even picked up his phone and Googled

Denver airport conspiracy theories, apparently, they had secret unground bunkers to house the elites in case of economic collapse or nuclear holocaust. It was like he was trying to save me from something the way he explained these things to me. In the article he found, there were scary looking pictures of weird artwork from the airport. One picture had a military-looking man wearing a gas mask and holding a long sword in one hand and an AK-47 in the other. At the man's feet were kids who had died, and a white dove (which signified peace) dead as well. The other picture had trees burning from some sort of solar flare and children crying over open caskets. In that painting, in the corner, was a letter that Wale zoomed in on for me to read.

The letter said -
"I was once a little child
who longed for the other worlds.
But I am no more a child
For I have known fear.

> I have learned to hate …….
> How tragic, then, is youth
> which lives with enemies,
> with gallows ropes.
> Yet, I still believe
> I only sleep today
> that I'll wake up
> a child again and
> start to laugh
> and play."

The letter made me feel a bit cold, and even more frightened than I was earlier. It was around 1AM and we were still having this weird but interesting talk, but now we had moved on to talking about the government and the Area 51 scientific bases. The Area 51 base, as Wale told me, was a Nevada Test and Training Range. However, it was mainly used to make weapons and test aliens that had been caught. He went further to say the government had a plan, and he Googled some things on his phone and passed it to me to read. The website had a page that talked about a certain book, and the section they took from this particular book had all the government plans laid out in the open. I read it closely.

Table of Plans

Start these actions

1. Make the people uninformed or unaware
2. Keep them occupied with bills, politics and more
3. Separate the family unit
4. Give more credits and promote less cash
5. Expose the sacredness of the church
6. Devalue the currency

To Create these results

1. It ensures less popular organizations
2. It makes them have very few defenses
3. Control the educational system of the younger ones
4. it lures people into personal pleasures without self-control and aids more data for the system
5. It destroys the faith in the church system

6. Creates a sense of doubt in the American people

Further Details

Media Outlets - Keeps people distracted from the actual issues.

Jobs – Under this section the people are meant to be very occupied that they have no time to think of anything else than work. Basically working 9 to 5 just to stay alive.

Entertainment – Entertainment is dumb down compared to previous years.

Education System – Children are educated at a lower level and are not taught the skills they actually need to survive.

After I read this I started to have a different outlook on life. That night I had to put a stop to Wale's lectures about the mysteries of the world. We lay in silence and just cuddled looking up into the skies, looking at the stars. Eventually the mosquitoes chased us away from the field and we decided to go back home to the more relaxed setting of our bed.

Chapter 25

Wale seemed to be one of those individuals who just loved adventure, and I say that because the next day he planned a kayaking trip for us. I agreed to go but had no idea what I was signing up for until I got to the location. Once we parked, Wale asked me to leave literally everything the car in case we fell in the water. When he said that, I wanted to back out, but after a moment's hesitation, I resumed walking very slowly behind him. The place looked like a shrine from a village back in Nigeria, one where native doctors have weird symbols and scary looking scars covering their faces, praising false gods. As Wale made the kayaking arrangements, all I could think about were the crocodiles, alligators, and snakes that could be in the water. At one point I thought that if there was an anaconda in the water I could lose my life on this kayaking trip.

Once Wale had paid for the kayaking fees, the person in charge gave us some basic instructions on paddling with the sticks along with basic information on the currents and a few other tips. Judging by the way he dressed and spoke, he seemed to be a local who grew up out there in the country. The instructor gave us life jackets to wear as we carried our paddles to the edge of the river where the boats were tied to a tree. When I looked at the river, I could see how fast the current was moving and immediately froze up.

Wale: "What's wrong?"

Me: "Um, I don't know if I can do this, the river is so wide."

Instructor: "It seems so, but you will fine, trust me."

Me: "Umm . . ."

Wale: "C'mon, get in."

Instructor: "Are you entering the same boat?"

Me: "Yes."

Wale: "No!"

Me: "No?"

Wale: "If we take the same boat you wouldn't get the full experience, c'mon!"

Me: "It looks scary!"

Wale: "Just get in."

As I glanced back, I saw the instructor had left, I was doubting that Wale knew what he was doing. I tried to get into the boat, but before I knew what was happening the boat had shifted, and I tumbled and fell straight into the water. The boat started to float off, but Wale caught it before the fast current took it away. I ran straight to the side of the river, screaming for the instructor to come back, all I could think was there was a snake or some sort of animal in the water. Wale stood beside the upside down boat giving me a look of disappointment.

Funke: "I don't think I can do this, I can't even swim!"

Wale: "You stood in the boat instead of sitting down, of course you were going to fall down!!!"

Funke: "Why are you screaming at me?"

Wale: "I'm not screaming at you! C'mon just relax and get in! You can do this."

I was overwhelmed by a series of mixed emotions and wanted to break down and cry right on the spot. On one hand, I thought that if I went any further with this kayaking thing I would probably die, but on the other I thought if I didn't go Wale would be so disappointed in me he might want to break up. I should have just researched what kayaking meant before agreeing to it.

Finally, I decided to get into the boat and go for the scary ride. I took a deep breath before sitting down, stretching the paddle sticks out, and following Wale's lead. The current was strong and at one point we came very close to a big branch sticking out of the water, it was a miracle we got past it without hitting it.

Lord knows if I had hit that branch I would have tumbled out and drowned, because by that point we had reached the deep water where my feet wouldn't touch the ground.

After a few minutes I started to get the hang of things, and actually raced Wale to the end where we were supposed to park and return our boats. As we raced we didn't see a single other person, so we decided to kiss right in the middle of the river where the current were a little slower. That kiss was simple and beautiful, right in the middle of nature with calm surroundings and only the sound of running river water.

Finally, we got to where we were supposed to park the boat, and after doing so well you would think I would have been able to end in a better way. I stopped alright, but forgot the "no standing in the boat" part, and again I tumbled out, only to get covered in fresh river water from my head down to my toes like I was being baptized. Good thing I hadn't brought my phone along.

      The kayaking had been slightly scary, but overall a great experience and in the end I was very grateful that I got to share that moment with Wale. Although to be honest, I think next time I would rather go sky-diving than kayaking because at least I could see what I was about to land on!

Chapter 26

Wale decided we should just relax at home for the last few remaining days before I had to go back to Chicago. He started to plan an elaborate house dinner and told his roommates about it. He called a few other friends to come over, and suddenly it was starting to become a house party before my eyes. One particular call I figured out was to his weed delivery man. I got a very judgmental look on my face, I always felt like weed made you go crazy and lose it.

Wale explained that we'd never hurt anyone, that it cured sickness and was more medicinal and for relaxation. He told me that normally he smoked it with a rolled-up paper, but that night he wanted to try to bake it, and he asked me to give it a try. Wale said everyone was going to participate in taking the weed, so we could all laugh and have a great time.

Once dinner was made, we all sat down

and started to talk. We had macaroni and cheese, mashed potatoes, greens, gravy with sweet potatoes, and chicken. We drank beer as we talked about celebrities and, one of Wale's favorite topics, the ancient aliens. After about an hour or so the brownie cake (with weed mixed in) was done. Everyone had a bite, including myself.

I didn't feel anything at first, and Wale even started to question if the weed delivery man had brought him a fake kind. As he was talking, I went behind him to have a few more pieces, I only took more because I loved chocolate and it didn't seem like anyone else wanted more of the brownies. I assumed the brownies were having no effect, so that was my green light to go ahead and take some more - a total of four pieces. That turned out to be a huge mistake.

We all sat back down on the floor, and I noticed I was laughing harder than normal, even just at the mention of just someone's name. I knew I was behaving strangely, but I couldn't stop myself. I laid down helplessly on the floor, my eyes became blurry and my vision was like I was wearing 3-D theatre glasses with red colors. Out of nowhere I started to scratch the floor, prowling like a cat on the rugs. By then it was just me and Wale left in the living room, so I thought that maybe if I slept it off, this weird behavior would go away. It didn't, but I didn't panic because at that point I thought it was just the beer we were drinking.

I felt my head banging and it felt like a giant kept kicking the walls of the whole building. I tapped Wale a few times to tell him, but all he did was laugh at me saying, "Oh shit, it's getting to you now, that's good." I rolled over to the corner of the wall like it was a cave and I was trying to stay warm. I must have blanked out because I had no idea how I got back to Wale's room from the living room. I looked around and saw him laying down just smiling at me, it was the weirdest thing ever. We both were super high from the brownie, so it became an every man for himself episode as he clearly wasn't in the right state of mind to help me out. My body started to feel hot, I couldn't seem to sit straight, I was itching, grabbing my head, and using my hands to physically open my eyes wide. The more I did this, the hotter my body seemed and my head was banging.

I sat up and looked around, and Wale asked me: "You good?"

Me: "No! No! This house is too hot! Oh my God!"

Wale: "No, the weather is cool, it's that good good stuff talking through you, just relax."

Me: "I said no, it's hot! Turn the AC on."

Wale: "Now you tripping, lay down on my chest."

Funke: "Hold on, I'm coming."

Suddenly, I got up and walked towards the living room, my eyes were blurry and my head banging. I don't know what I was doing, it was like I was being controlled by a higher person. It was the craziest thing ever as I walked towards the door and ran outside with no shoes or slippers. I roamed the parking lot in Wale's complex, just touching the cars all parked in the lot. My mind kept telling me to get in a car to go get help, I may be dying from the brownie mix, so I tried to force one of them open, within seconds Wale come out and pulled me back in. It was a struggle and he had to carry me up the stairs back into the apartment. Once we got in he closed the doors, set me down and took me back to his room.

Wale: "Oh my God, this weed really got you fucked up!"

Me: "Yes, yes, the man."

Wale: "What?"

Me: "The man, the weed man."

Wale: "What about him?"

Me: "Come closer, I can't say it loud, he will kill me."

Wale: "Chill out! Who is gonna kill you?"

Me: "The man, I said the man, listen, please, the man."

Wale: "You are tripping, what are you talking about?"

Me: "Let me say it in your ear, come closer please."

Wale: "You scaring me, just say it where you are."

Me: " okay the man put something . . ."

Wale: "Huh?"

Me: "The man put something in the weed."

Wale: "The man always bring me weed, stop talking like this, you freaking me out."

Me: " okay I'm sorry now, I said I'm sorry, please don't be angry."

Wale: "Chill out!!"

Me: " okay I'm sorry, I won't shout, please please . . ."

The reason I was saying sorry was because my mind had all sorts of things going through it at once, and I thought maybe Wale planned with the weed man to put something in the brownie, just around the pieces I took. I thought if I made too much noise he might beat me out of anger and frustration from trying to calm me down, so I kept saying, "I'm sorry" to calm him down. I sat there for a few seconds, but I just couldn't sit still and Wale seemed to be getting more and more irritated and angry.

Me: "Please can we call the police?"

Wale: "For what?"

Me: "I think the man . . . yes the man, put something in the brownie like strong Kush."

Wale: "Stop this, you fucking annoying me."

Me: "Stop getting mad, it's my first time, please, my head is paining me."

Wale: "Just relax, you making it a big deal."

Me: "Oh my God it's hot, please, I need to talk to the police to help me so I don't die!"

Wale: "Nah, you not gonna ruin my record or get me in trouble, so sit down here and relax. We will both go to jail because we both black. Just forget it."

Me: "Argh!! Please, please my head!"

After that I started wandering around in a circle talking to myself, my words didn't seem to make sense anymore. I asked Wale very forward questions, I forced him to say things he wasn't ready for. I don't know why I did it, but in my mind I thought that him saying those things would convince me he wasn't gonna kill me and get rid of the body so as not to get him in trouble for the illegal weed.

Me: "Please tell me!"

Wale: "Tell you what?"

Me: "Just listen, please."

Wale: "OKAY."

Me: "okay, listen, listen . . ."

Wale: "Yes, I'm listening."

Me: "Do you love me?"

Wale: "Oh wow!"

Funke: "Please say it."

Wale: "I can't say it."

Funke: "Why? Why?"

Wale: "I can't say it this way, please stop this."

Funke: "Why, you don't love me?"

Wale: "I wanted to say it at the right moment, but not like this"

Funke: "Say it . . . please!"

Wale: "Alright then, I love you."

Funke: " okay, okay, you're not angry?"

Wale: "No."

My head started to itch and I felt hot again. I went into the bathroom to splash water on my face thinking I would be okay. I did it multiples times, and even tried to count, but got stuck on number five. I had no clue what number was next after five, so I just repeated five over and over. My head still hadn't stopped banging, so I jumped in the shower and let the water run over my whole body.

I was in the shower fully clothed, washing myself with soap all over myself in my clothes. Wale got in the shower and tried to stop me, and the next thing I knew I found myself on the bed. I was now in shorts and a t- shirt under the blankets, I closed my eyes and saw myself on a stage performing in front of millions. That night was horrific, sad, and terrifying.

The next morning, I had a little better control over where I was and what I was doing, but Wale didn't seem to have slept at all. He kept staring at me, constantly asking if I was okay. I remember asking him why he had black marks all over his face, and he said I was responsible. I have no memory of ever hitting him and I would have sworn on my life that I hadn't. I must have been a monster.

I didn't remember anything from the time I got in the shower to the time I found myself laying in the bed. I stayed in bed for two days straight just drinking liquids and eating a few spoonfuls of food which Wale fed me. Once I had recovered, I felt terrible. His room was a mess, things were scattered everywhere, but I didn't remember messing it up. Despite that crazy incident, Wale still dropped me off at the airport, and had lunch with me just before I got on the plane. He hugged and kissed me before I went through the gates, but I feared it was a kind of permanent goodbye, as he gave me a look like I would never see his face again.

Chapter 27

On one particularly beautiful day in Chicago I decided to check out some modeling auditions online. I was able to find a few. One in particular had an extremely professional looking advertisement, as well as ads on other social media platforms, and some mentions on the radio station. The audition they were holding were for all ages, men and women of all races available for modeling, acting, and voiceover work.

The audition event was all the way in Rosemont near O'Hare International Airport. When I arrived, the hall was filled with people, mostly parents with their kids. The girls had a mean look and the boys had something I called a thirsty look. I was extremely nervous thinking about auditioning in front of everyone in the hall, but once my number was called they just took me into an office for a quick interview where they asked about what experience I had. After I answered the questions I had to hold up a piece of paper with my name and birthdate on it, while they took a Polaroid picture and stapled it all together. After that we had a quick talk about how you shouldn't ever pay a modeling agency to model for them, however it would cost $600 for them to find me an audition, and $55 a shoot to take professional photos for a modeling portfolio. They found a way to get money from you some way, somehow and I learnt the hard way. I paid for a photographer from their company to help me build my portfolio so I could pursue my modeling dreams.

When we met at the location, he brought many props for me to pose with. I wore a white dress and reclined on a couch in an elegant pose looking like a very wealthy lady. I also took a picture on the back of a motorcycle wearing just my bra and panties, which was very uncomfortable, but I told myself that's just how it is in the world of modeling. I did some other poses, including headshots, switching out my clothing a few times, but a week went by, and the photographer never emailed me any pictures. He never returned my calls, he just disappeared, and the company kept saying he was on vacation.

But I didn't let that stop me from pursuing my modeling dreams. I had always wanted to model, and often day-dreamed about doing print ads for major magazines. I pictured myself at different photo shoots, wearing different wigs, lying in front of the famous Sphinx in Egypt, or on a plane, or somehow even lying on water rather than walking on it. I knew all the super models who were walking the Paris runways, and I did plenty of research about what fashion was trendy in New York, Paris, London and Milan. I read books that talked about color trends and silhouettes. I wished I could be more fashion forward in my personal style, but I was brought back to reality when I remembered that I still didn't have a job.

    I responded to an ad for a runway modeling audition for a local designer in Chicago, and she chose me to walk in her show. I remember posting the event on my social media page because the designer said she got extra money for every seat we could fill. The big day finally came and I strutted my stuff in the show and met a lot of people. To my surprise, Wale came to meet me backstage. He had driven all the way from Atlanta to Chicago to come attend my first modeling show, and I was truly grateful.

That night, instead of making him stay at a hotel, I invited him to stay with me, but it was a poor decision. I thought Mark would be out driving his taxi all night, so I told Wale to get comfortable. I was cooking and Wale was in the shower when the living room door opened, and before I knew it. Mark had entered. Wale must have forgotten that I told him Mark stays in the living room, and when Mark opened the door with a friend of his from church the first thing they saw was Wale totally butt naked from the shower. It was very embarrassing and remained uncomfortable even once Wale had left back to go back to Atlanta. Mark started to act differently in the house, he started to hint that he had found someone to marry and was going to move her in. So that was my cue to start looking for a new place to live.

Chapter 28

I had to move in with my mum who was temporarily staying in the south side of Chicago. I stopped going to school for a while in order to find a job and make ends meet and save some money so I could be financially stable. Living with my mum was not the best situation, but all my other options were out. She had strong opinions, and she wanted things her way because it was her house.

From time to time she would sit me down and ask if I was ever going to call my sister to try and close up the distance between us, but I would always say no. My mother liked to pick and pick at every little mistake I made in the house. I think she was just bored and angry that she wasn't in control of her surroundings as she would have been in Nigeria. She also didn't have many friends, she had fought with almost everyone I knew from my childhood days.

The week before I moved in with her she fought a friend over twenty-five dollars. Mind you, she is nowhere close to being poor; she is the landlord for four spaces she is building houses on in addition to her being a high-ranking police officer, she only fought out of greed, every penny mattered to her.

I had to work to be able to have some personal money coming in, because it was a constant war asking my mother for money. Anytime I asked her for something she would start to list everything that I owed her, including the ticket money she was always asking me for. She even included all the birthday and Mother's Day gifts I had failed to give her, conveniently forgetting those were times when I had no job. I went over to a government building that helped people look for work. I skipped the regular process, which took a whole day, and just took a sheet of paper that listed companies that were hiring from the job board. I flipped through the pages, skipping over food industry, retail industry, security work, and finally came to a halt at the health worker ads. I had seen a lot of health worker ads recently, so I went to go apply at a company down the road.

I decided to apply for the position of Home Health Aide, it was the easiest one to get and make fast money. At the front desk I given a checklist of things to bring in before I could attend the free training classes, including medical scrubs and white sneakers. However, a physical was required along with two work references. Luckily the medical insurance I had covered the physical test I had to do at the hospital. I had to get everything checked including Rubella and taking a drug test. I went back and forth so many times that I got frustrated. They would send me back to the doctor saying he didn't include the needle size when they could simply call him and ask. They must have wanted his writing in the forms I guessed so I didn't fight it and just did as they wanted. There were a lot of rules and they inspected us as soon as we walked in the door. If your nails were too long you would be sent back home, if you had big hoops or long earrings you would be sent back home, if your hair wasn't in a bun you would be sent back home.

The training classes were super intense, we took a test every single day for 2 weeks. We learned everything from emergency calls to taking blood pressure, colostomy patients, diabetic patients, and how to transfer a patient from a bed to a wheel chair using a hoyer lift. We even learned how to turn bed-bound patients every 2 hours to avoid getting bed sores.

At the beginning of the class we started with 20 people and by the end of the two weeks we were down to only nine, the others had all broken the rules or failed a test. After the two week training period was over we were given our initial assignments. My first case was working with a stroke patient who needed assistance with walking to the bathroom, feeding, bathing, dressing, and getting in and out of the bed.

On my first day a nurse came along to show me the ropes. She instructed me on everything from how to wash my hands properly to how to dispose of my gloves, and what to do if the patient fell down. It was during the nurse's visit that I got know that she was the mother to the receptionist who gave me the application on the first day for the training. The home health aide also told me the person who owned the company was Nigerian and she had all four of her kids working in the office. That was what we called keeping the money within the family. She also told me that whenever I heard them using the word "Administrator" that it's really the owner of the company who always hides from seeing her workers. The company had a history of holding on to Home Health Aides Certificates to restrict them from working elsewhere in the city. They even stylishly without being direct told us that if we applied elsewhere we would not be allowed to ever come back to their company. In fact, they would at times have 4-hour cases and if we didn't take the case they would write us up. It was ridiculous.

  I saw it all working as a home health aide, the good, the bad and the crazy. There was the time I went to a client's house and was told to take off my shoes and leave my coat and bags by the door. Now normally we home health aides have to wear our shoes to be safe from sharp objects or fluids on the floor. So, when the client wanted me to walk around in just my socks, I refused and called my supervisor to tell her I wasn't comfortable working there.

Before I could even gather my things to leave, the client's wife started waving a broom at me to get me to hurry up. I was professional, but I did tell her, "Mam I am leaving your house as I have also told the supervisor, but please, I advise that you don't let that broom touch me!"

One time I took care of a child who ripped my shirt at the park in front of everyone. After that the agency started to enforce the rule about only wearing scrubs to work and no necklaces or chains. But it was primarily the clients' relatives who made the job seem like Hell. I was often called "disgusting" or told that my skin "looked nasty" as a more polite way of saying "Nigga". What choice did I have though? I reported everything to my supervisor, but I still remained on the case because it was hard to get another job.

In the Home Health aide field if you left one

case, sometimes it could take a whole month before you could get another one. The good side was we often got paid to literally do nothing at times. Some patients were able to walk, bathe, and do most things for themselves - all you had to do was keep them from falling and be good company. On cases like that a Home Health Aide could sit and watch TV with the client all day, sleep when the client slept, and get paid for an easy shift. Overnight jobs were rare to get, but if you could get one, you would literally just come and sleep near the client.

The ones I hated the most were the live-ins, where you had to live with the client for four days out of the week. You weren't allowed to leave them at all until the fourth day, you had to cook, bathe, and do everything right there in their house. I was able to save a lot of money though. And as soon as my mum calculated what my check was, she told me to start paying rent in addition to the gas, cable, and light bills.

Chapter 29

I had been thinking of traveling to go see Wale again. We had been texting and calling each other a lot, but hadn't seen each other since the incident at Mark's. Things seemed to have changed, the connection between us was a dry Sahara desert. I knew he was going through a lot, his family was giving him hell, but I didn't understand why he had shoved me to the side and didn't want to open up to me. He wasn't caring like he had been before, he hardly checked on me. Sometimes when I called he wouldn't pick up. If I texted I wouldn't get a reply until hours, or sometimes days later. I figured he was probably just over me, and I wanted to find out.

Me: "When do you have break from school so I can come see you?"

Wale: "I really can't say yet."

Me: "You sure you're okay? You seem different these days."

Wale: "How so?"

Me: "Maybe it's just me, I feel you are quieter."

Wale: "I'm good"

Me: "What is really going on? You are totally shutting down on me."

Wale: "Nothing."

Me: "Wow. Wale, I'm trying here, this is not fair at all."

Wale: "How?"

Me: "Idk anymore, my head hurts. All you say is "nothing" and "I'm good."

Wale: "And I have told you - I'm good."

Me: "Your actions don't say so. These days when I text you, you reply late and that's usually only when I text you multiple times. When you do respond, there is a tone to it. I hate to keep nagging, but it's what I notice. I feel like I'm texting a random guy who doesn't wanna be bothered."

Wale: "Now I have a tone? I get numb, and when I am numb I act like a stranger."

Me: "How are you a stranger?"

Wale: "I don't act or sound the same,"

Me: "Gosh, you are taking my words and misinterpreting them. All I am saying is I just feel a gap. Something is bothering you."

Wale: "Things bother me every day, that's life. Talking about them changes nothing."

Me: "It may not change it, but at least I will have an idea of what's bothering you. Do you think I enjoy being left out in the dark? Surprisingly it may be something I can help with. You never know."

Wale: "Thanks, but you need to stop."

Me: "Stop caring?"

Wale: "Yes."

Me: "How can you say that?"

Wale: "Because I'd be okay."

Me: "It's rubbing off on me sadly. You don't get it. I wish you would just let me in just a little bit. I don't have to know everything."

Wale: "Not my style."

Me: " Okay and you're entitled to that. So, for me to stop nagging continuously I need to understand something. Forgive me, I don't even know how to ask this. But do you need space? I don't wanna be a stress factor for you at this time. Expecting a cheerful message, etc."

Wale: "I'm just in a bad state of mind. Where everything and anything has stopped exciting me. You worry too much."

Me: " Okay I may not be able to change that, but I would like to take you out somewhere when I'm around or when I see you, cool?"

Wale: "Where?"

Me: "Umm, I could search a couple of places nearby."

Wale: "No, never mind, don't worry yourself."

The next day we went back and forth once more.

Wale: "I'm having mood swings."

Me: "I'm hurt because of how you are acting towards

me and communicating with me."

Wale: "I'm not talking with anybody. The fact that I'm responding to you is a huge deal. I get mood swings."

Me: "Wow! Even though we getting closer, you have to realize that some things about you I am still learning, so when you pull away on me like that you can't blame me for being concerned or lost."

Wale: "I can go numb for a month or more. If you can't handle it, then maybe you might want to withdraw from getting attached to me."

Me: "Sigh. Don't talk to me like that!"

Wale: "It's the blunt truth."

Me: "I know it is. From my end it just seemed different. That's why I couldn't let it go. I'm starting to understand what's going on. I thought you were dismissing me, just stuff was going through my mind each time."

Wale: "Look, I'm not in the state of mind to worry about how "my silence" is affecting you, because this isn't about you."

Me: "No need to explain further. I did some reading and I totally get it. It's not about me, right now you have to worry about you and I'm here if you need me for anything."

Wale: "Thanks."

Me: "Anytime dear. Thanks for opening up a little tonight, to help me understand."

Wale: "K"

After that I didn't hear from him for two days until he finally messaged me saying he went to a friend's party. I was like "wow" in my head. "You could have at least told me." is what I texted in response. I didn't understand how someone could go from being emotionally numb to suddenly attending a party.

Wale: "I'm having mood swings."

Me: "It's so unfair for you to shut me out in this manner. I care about you, but it hurts the way you have communicated with me these past few days. It's like you don't care about me anymore. You have been saying you're in a numb state for days now, is that all I get as an explanation. I'm not happy at all. To be honest, I am hurt, I never thought you would put me in a hurtful atmosphere like this. Even on the days that I am mad or worried about personal things, I try my best to not make you feel neglected. I don't feel comfortable shutting you out for long, in fact I tell you a bit about what's bothering me. I don't see you or talk to you much, and all I get are a few words when we do talk. I am not a block of wood Wale, I have feelings. I wanna be there for you emotionally, financially, however the case. I wanna share your happiness, your pain, and all the rest. Treating me like this with such distance, like I'm a stranger, is messed up. Every day I look forward to hearing from you, and it's been clouds lately. How can you even feel comfortable with this level of communication? Gosh I'm so angry, I'm not your enemy for crying out loud!"

Wale: "I'm fine, I never said you were my enemy. I'd prefer to have this conversation in person, but the sooner the better. Remember how when we first met I told you I had just gotten out of a relationship and wasn't ready to get into anything new? Well I feel like going forward I have over- reached with you, led you to believe that I can give more than my friendship by my actions. For that I am sorry. The last few weeks of my quiet time I have had time to reflect and see how things are playing out, and if I don't stop it now I will only end up hurting you because I can't give that part of myself to anybody right now. This is one of the reasons I have not been speaking much or traveling to see you lately, because you have gotten too used to the idea of my presence. I enjoy hanging out with you too, but in the long run I will only be holding you back from people who can actually make you happy. I hope you understand, and I really wanted to clear the air before it got deeper."

    I felt so hurt after I read this, and I couldn't reply for about two days. I woke up each morning with a heavy heart and tears rolling down my face. My chest lurched from the memories whenever I looked at his name on my phone screen or even thought of him. I couldn't eat, and I kept tossing and turning on my bed, over and over and over. Thinking of him squeezed my heart so hard I felt like I would suffocate. All I could think about was what I might have done to make him want to withdraw. Love had me so confused, I had no confidence to move on.

Finally, I texted Wale that I would like to end this properly in person. I bought a ticket to go see him, but two days before I was going to board the plane I stopped hearing from him, his phone was completely switched off. I remember being at the gate dialing his number over and over, until the lady from the airline had to tell me they were closing the door.

I kept on dialing even once I got to my seat because it was bizarre for me to be flying without having heard from the person I was going to see. Just as they said, "Switch off your phone," Wale picked up only to say, "You already told me when you were coming, I was busy with stuff. Calm down." This time I stayed at a hotel, not in his place.

When we finally saw each other in person we expressed how much we missed each other. One thing led to another, and it happened. My tears fell down to the bed sheets, but Wale calmed me with his lips on mine. Gently he touched my waist and I looked up, hoping to see a future once again in his eyes. I didn't know if any of this meant that we would be getting back together, but it didn't matter.

  I put my legs over his legs and as I climbed on top of him I felt the heat of his manhood against my feminine part. Our waists met at a direct angle that could either cause a volcanic eruption or a bodily heat wave. Our lips opened a passageway for our tongues to meet. He unbuttoned my shirt and squeezed a handful of my breast squeezing it with a tender appeal that took me to another dimension. I closed my eyes and bent my body back, letting my hair dangle to the floor.

  I sat on Wale's lap as he leaned forward and locked his succulent wet lips on my upright nipple. My body shook as he ignited a sensual light that made me feel like I was being revived from a trance, like I hadn't been alive until that moment. My body and soul were up for bid between his lips, his hand, and his manhood. A little part of me felt like we should attend a church vigil because tonight's event would be the ultimate sin. Tapping into my overwhelming and dangerous lust, he scanned my thighs with his eyes and then with his hands. I submitted my body to him. I trusted him with all of me. Body to body, tongue to tongue, I began to climb his mountain.

His manhood craved the warmth inside me. As he started to enter me I took a deep breath and swallowed a little prayer.

Pain is pleasure and I had to surrender my body to it all. He pushed deep inside me and grabbed my neck like he would never let go. In that moment I knew that I was on a journey through an endless path of satisfaction beyond ordinary levels. His influence set me on a mission to release my inner wild side. A wild side destined for fun with no cause to look back.

That night was breathtaking, I never

thought I would do things like I did that night. He inspired me with ideas and filled me up with creative juices. When he finally slept beside me I grabbed my diary and wrote something very nasty, yet very creative. I called it "Into My Scriptures."

Into My Scriptures

My nipples are like two heavenly antennae that should be given proper acknowledgment. It's the rightful thing for you to get on your knees before my altar. Stick your tongue between my two chapters, feel free to support your movement with your hands setting them apart like the Red Sea. My moaning and humming are the chapters in the new era that could be quoted for salvation.

The writings on my thighs represent the times you have signed in and signed out for your passionate shift and have piped me down tremendously. At this moment I want you to come into thy temple. Conquer my body and pin me across the wall. Shatter my pillars and cast away my doubts. Administer your potential into my body, let my waterfall dispense down my thighs and unto the marble floor.

It was like day and night, things had changed between us once again. I thought the lovemaking had changed his mind on where we stood, things were going well, until a particular day when I was waiting in the hotel while Wale was at work. I had received a phone call from my mother.

Mother: "Where are you?"

Me: "I'm in Atlanta."

Mother: "Oh? Did you tell me you were traveling?"

Me: "I thought I did when you asked me to buy some groceries."

Mother: "You told me, but you didn't tell me exactly when."

Me: "I'm sorry, I thought you knew."

Mother: "Well, I just called to let you know that I am tired of paying bills in this country, I want to go back to Nigeria, so you need to find a place to move to."

Me: "Oh wow, but when?"

Mother: "What kind of foolish question is that? I can leave anytime: tomorrow, tonight, anytime, just be ready. I refuse to be using my own money to be paying rent while one stupid child is traveling all over enjoying herself."

Me: " Wow."

Mother: " Wow what?"

Me: "Nothing, I will find my way."

Mother: "Well, while I am still around I have decided to increase the rent. You have plenty of money to be traveling, so I'm sure you can afford it."

Me: "I don't have plenty of money, I cannot afford it!"

Mother: "That is your business, and if you can't afford it, get ready to find your things outside on the road."

She hung up the phone right after she made that statement. The conversation ruined my mood, and I just didn't want to respond to anymore. It took me hours to even reply to Wale, and when I did I told him I was frustrated. I didn't understand how my mother could not be supportive at all. She picked fights with me all the time. She was the person that had told me to move in with her to be able to save money to pick-myself up properly and be financially stable to move out on my own once school was over.

Wale left work early when I told him I was suicidal. He came over to have a talk with me, but I was just tired of talking in general and especially of rehashing all my family struggles. We sat on the bed in silence. I didn't speak and just kept telling him, "Don't worry, I'll be fine." He started to get mad that I wasn't talking, but when I finally forced myself to start talking.

He said I was complaining like a kid and that I should be used to my mother by now. I was emotional, and I was crying, and he had the nerve to tell me I was acting like a baby? That my crying was becoming irritating? He didn't even lean over to hold me, he was so cold that out of nowhere I said, "No one cares about me, I am just tired, I just wanna die." Those words pissed him off - he got angry and walked out on me. I didn't understand what just happened, so I texted him.

Me: "What you did just now seriously hurt me. Nice to know that you are comfortable walking out on me."

Wale: "GREAT to know you feel comfortable wasting my time with that whole 'no one cares about me' crap. You think nobody cares about you? Be that way, I'm done."

Me: "Wow. I wasn't wasting your time. You got mad as soon as I began to talk, I just seem to make you so mad. You couldn't even calm down to talk further, instead you walked out on me and slammed the door. Is that how you wanna treat me? Cool. Your reaction and anger makes me afraid to open up further. I don't understand why I make you so mad so quickly. You really hurt me walking out on me like that. I'm a fucking human being that has been hurt all my life, and for you to drop out on me in the middle of me talking like that wasn't cool. I would never walk out on you like that, no matter what. I'm seriously hurt, I wouldn't have imagined you ever doing that to me.

Wale: "I will only tell you this much. In this life we are responsible for ourselves, Nobody can save you, only you can. There are two types of people, the ones that turn their pain into power, and the kind that let the pain kill them. You need to decide which one of those people you want to be. I am sorry, but I don't believe in weakness, and I don't throw or attend pity parties, take the time to find your voice and strength."

Me: "That's not fair and a bit harsh. If you cared you would never walk out on me, no matter what. When you refused to talk, telling me you were emotionally numb, I stuck by you for days. Even when you gave me the cold shoulder, I never ran out on you. Nobody asked for your pity, just your shoulders to lean on and your ears to listen, that's all I needed. I don't know where this tough love is coming from, but I know this is not how you spoke to me when we first met. I'm not stupid or weak, I'm a caring person and deserve the same in return."

    A lot of people may say I was a fool, that I was weak and a sucker for love. I don't know what I was, but I was so hurt at that moment that I got on my knees and prayed to the Lord. I had never before prayed to God on behalf of a relationship, Wale was the first ever. I asked God to help me melt his heart and make him loving like the way he was when we first met. But I didn't receive any text messages or calls after the last one I sent. I spent the remaining nights alone in Atlanta. When it was time to leave, I went to the airport alone. I cried all the way to the airport, I cried at the gate waiting to board, and I cried the entire flight back to Chicago. Once I was home, I grabbed my diary again and wrote my pain down onto paper.

The night before I wish I had died. I had prepared a suicidal letter for those who were supposed to be there for me and claimed to love me. Nothing will change it seems. I wonder why pain chooses to run through my blood stream. Depression has placed its dark blanket upon my life, I can't remember the last time I actually smiled from within. I fake smiles because it's so much easier than explaining why I'm sad. I wear black clothes because my life is a funeral. I wake up wanting to kill myself, and I go to bed wondering why I didn't. The roses around me have turned black and my source of joy has dipped its complete self in the pool of sorrow. Everybody has a chapter they don't read out loud.

My chapter stayed bottled in like most, but the pain within my soul bleeds on a daily basis. I was told to suck it up and that everyone has problems, but in reality, no one has time to simply listen. When my joy was taken away I was told to suck it up. When I was raped I was told to hush for the integrity of the family name, and to suck it up, that I wouldn't be the first to be raped. These words were read to me like Bible scriptures on a daily basis. When I sought for the help of a therapist to listen and advise me, my loved ones told me therapy is of the Western culture, that it's only for white people. Black people and Africans go to church and pray is what my loved ones told me. I am weak when I tell my neighbor I have pain. I am irritating when I cry to my partner. I am to apologize for being emotional. I am an adult, so I must not complain about what's giving me frustration. I can't even cry upon the shoulders of someone without them telling me to suck it up and be perfect before the presence of mankind. Life as we know it is no more like the good old days where there was someone to be the ear you need or the shoulders for you to lean on.

Chapter 30

Several months passed, but it never got any easier dealing with the heartbreak and living with a mother I couldn't even ask for advice or speak to about anything personal. My job started to get annoying, it wasn't like the clients were giving me a tough time - I was just mad at the world because I had had my heart broken. Every time I looked at my phone I hoped he would call, but that was just a fantasy, in reality Wale had moved on.

My mother started to give me even more hell than usual, it was like she turned into someone I didn't recognize. Whenever the first of the month arrived she would come knocking on my door at 5AM asking for the rent in nothing but cash. I would have to get up and go to the ATM in the middle of the night. Sometimes I couldn't get her the rent money on the first, usually because one of my health aide clients had switched to another provider, but she just said that wasn't her problem. If she didn't get the money on time she would lock the doors and send me a text telling to me bring the rent money or find somewhere else to sleep until I did.

One of the craziest things she did was to grab all the dirty pots and plates I had left in the sink when I rushed to work in the morning and put them in my bed so the stew stains and greasy leftovers rubbed all over my bedsheets. Imagine coming home from a long day of work and jumping under the covers only to hit your head on a pot placed under your bedsheet. I would get so upset, I would fling the pots out into the hallway or sometimes toss them out the window into the streets where my mum would see them when she was out on her errands. I was lucky they didn't hit anyone.

That's when things really started to get heated in the house. She would stand in front of the door demanding the rent money saying, "I will not leave here until I receive the rent money, if you want to beat me go ahead and beat me foolish girl, bastard bitch, child of the devil, fool!" It seemed silly to be blocking the entrance while she demanded her money when she knew I needed to go out to the ATM to get it for her.

My mother started to intentionally mess with me by stealing things I needed like the house keys or the TV remote. One time she came back from an outing, walked up to me, and grabbed my box of pizza shouting, "You selfish human being, you are eating pizza alone in this house when the bathroom needs cleaning. Did you bring a housemaid from Nigeria to come and clean for you?"

Before I could reply she tossed my box of pizza into the garbage. I could have walked away and ignored her, I could have called a friend to calm me down over the phone, I could have gone to clean the bathroom to get her off my back, but the anger that had been building inside me had reached its maximum point, and I lost my mind.

I started to scream and shout saying things I should never have said like, "Why are you so wicked and angry at the world? If you are frustrated with yourself then find a fucking way to deal with it and stop making my life hell! What have I done to you? OMG I am sick and tired of this shit!"

As I was screaming at her I started to break things and fling food around. I broke the dishes, I broke the kitchen dining table, I broke the decorations, I broke the wall clock, and lastly, I broke the TV. While all this was going on she went into the bathroom to hide and call the cops. She came back out telling me, "I will deal with you in the American way, I should have aborted you when I had the opportunity. What a curse in form of a child. You will sleep in jail!"

The cops came and listened to both of our stories. I explained, "How can I pay for rent when for the past two weeks all I have collected is $86 dollars? Am I also supposed to still get a Metro transit card and eat with that little money?"

The first police officer looked shocked when he saw the check and asked if I had shown it to my mother. I said, "She told me she doesn't care." The other officer was kind of a jerk though because he told me I needed a plan to replace everything broken in the house otherwise my mother would take me to court.

The police had visited that apartment so many times it had become ridiculous, the next day the landlord told us if we called the police one more time he would throw us out. From then on I would still try and be friendly and greet mum, but she would ignore me like I didn't even exist, and would only communicate by writing things on paper or texting, even when we were both in the house at the same time. I think she took pleasure in watching me plead for forgiveness even though I was innocent.

Whenever family members called, they would never hear or believe my side of the story because in our culture the parents are always right. So, they would scold me or say, "Well it's is wrong to say your mother is wrong, you still have to beg for her forgiveness."

Chapter 31

The signs of pregnancy snuck in like a thief in the night –suddenly I started having dizzy spells and intense food cravings. I tried my best to hide them from my wicked mother, but nothing stays hidden for long - in the dark it will always come to light. I had been sleeping for days and days. Then one morning I was vomiting, and without knocking on the bathroom door, my mother walked in and grabbed my hair while my head was lowered in the sink. She grabbed it tight and pulled my head up until she could look me in my eyes only to say, "Not in this house, you will get rid of that bastard child." I did all I could do to fight her about aborting my child. She threatened me on so many occasions, trying to get me to have an abortion, but I just couldn't do it. Wherever Wale was, I am sure he had no idea he was about to be a father and I didn't even bother contacting him because I could not face more rejection and pain.

Months went by and I got an approval for a long leave from work. I had to cook for myself all throughout my pregnancy as mum assured me that she would not support me giving birth to 'Satan's kids'. I went to the hospital and delivered with not a single person by my bedside other than the doctor and nurse. I gave birth to twins, a boy and a girl and I named them Moses and Nihema.

I stared at my kids and had a flood of tears rush down my eyes. I hadn't smiled in a very long time, but I smiled at that first moment I held them. They were the best gifts ever given to me, even though I didn't get to keep them for too long, my mother had made sure of that.

My mother had called the psychiatric ward and showed them the diary she had stolen from my room filled with my depression notes and suicidal letters. She lied and told them I had confessed to wanting to kill my kids because the father hurt me, and that she feared I was suffering from postpartum depression. She even showed them the police reports she had made against me saying I was a very violent person.

    Luckily she didn't win despite her Oscar nominated role full of lies to the Child Protective Services. The pressure at home was intense, I feared for my kids and began staying up all night thinking my mother might poison them or smack them with something. I would run out the shower every time I heard them cry, thinking she was doing harm to them.

    My mother even increased the rent on account of my kids who she hated so dearly. Rather than being able to enjoy my children, I found myself totally soaked with frustration at my mother. Rather than being able to rest when my babies were finally sleeping, I was up in the living room arguing with her about their presence. One day I came home after a doctor's appointment with my kids only to find that the lock on the door had been changed. I inserted the key over and over, thinking I must be going crazy. I called mum about five times, but she didn't pick up, only sent me a text to say, "I think you and your bastard children need to live elsewhere, go and find another apartment please."

I was distraught standing at the door with my crying babies. Our neighbor must have gotten tired of them crying in the hallway as she had asked me to come and stay with her. Later that evening, as the babies were catching some sleep after I had breastfed them, my neighbor gently came up to me with a soft voice. I thought she was going to say her husband had seen a random lady with her breast out feeding her child in his living room and now wanted us out.

Instead, she started with off by saying, "It's not my business," and continued to explain that she had heard all the arguments. She asked "wouldn't you prefer your kids to be raised in a more stable and peaceful environment ?". Some people may have gotten defensive about this, but I listened to what she had to say. She raised some great points, and convinced me that I wouldn't be able to focus on my kids and give them what I wanted to without the support of my mother.

The two of us fighting every day could spark into something brutal or even worse. She gave me some information about adoption, and though I thought to myself that giving up my kids wasn't the best option I wanted, at the moment it was the only healthy thing for them. How could I raise them without a stable home environment? The government might help with food stamps and things but having a peaceful home is crucial.

The neighbor introduced me to a social worker who was furious that my mother was not supportive at all. She made it her personal priority to call me, even after her shift, to check on me and my kids. I guess sometimes the kindness of strangers can be more reliable than the kindness of your own family. The social worker sat me down at a park near her office for a long conversation, to make sure I knew what I was getting into by me giving up my kids for adoption. She told me having a baby out of wedlock often had a stigma attached, and that women like myself were often under pressure not to bring shame on theirfamilies, so they had no choice but to give up their babies for adoption.

Throughout the entire process I silently prayed that my mother's ice-cold heart would change towards me and my kids, but it never did. Finally, the day came when the social worker called and said that someone with a wealthy background had seen the pictures of my kids and wanted to take them in. I remember calling my mum from the taxi on the way to meet the social worker, desperately pleading with her to just let me take care of my kids in her home, I even promised not to ever ask her for anything to take of them. She kept silent until I was finished and then said, "Is this why you disturbed my sleep? Please give the kids away, it's the best thing," and she hung up the phone.

I had tears rolling down my eyes, and as I breastfed my kids for the very last time, my tears kept dropping on their faces. I was such a complete mess that the taxi driver let me hang out in his cab outside of the social worker's office and didn't even charge me anything. I never met my kid's new adoptive parents, but I was somewhat calm because I trusted that they would be in a loving, peaceful environment. I felt like I was moving in slow motion as I handed over Moses and Nihema and signed the adoption papers, smudging my signature with my tears.

I had just given away two human beings that came out of my womb, and I would probably never see them again. Their faces floated in my thoughts, I softly repeated their names to myself as I walked, knowing that if I said goodbye to them they wouldn't grasp what I was saying at their age. All I could do was hope that one day in the future I would be welcomed back into their life with a hug.

After that, a huge part of me shut down from the world, especially my family, specifically my mother. I just laid in bed thinking about my kids. I looked at their clothes and cuddled them like they were still there. In the middle of the night I would jump out of bed thinking I had overslept and hadn't changed their diapers, only to remember that they had been given up for adoption. I started to lose myself in a place of extreme madness and began sending random rants to my mother. She called the police and they took me to a psychiatric ward. In the psychiatric ward they took away all of my belongings like I was in prison. After about 30 minutes they called my name, and when the three doctors sat down across from me I knew exactly what was going on. They asked me if I wanted to do harm to myself, did I think of death, did I want to commit suicide, did I want to hurt others.

    I just said no to everything, but the truth was I wanted to kill myself because I was tired of the pain. I don't know if I truly would ever have picked up a knife and gone ahead with it, but I knew I couldn't just tell them the truth because in places like that once you started to say yes they will admit you to their facility like a prisoner. They could basically keep you against your will for months, you couldn't go out, you could only eat their kind of food, and they could treat you with complete disrespect. If you told them that you had an apartment you were paying for, they would just ignore your rants, they wouldn't care. It was exactly like a nursing home, with a wicked staff who smiled at you during the day and gave you mean looks after hours. They knew to hide from the cameras as they took off their shoes to whack you on your face, or place pills in your mouth to make you sleep it off.

Chapter 32

After giving the babies up, I moved out of my mother's place, as per her request, and randomly decided to move to Bloomingdale, Illinois to live as far from anyone I knew as possible. I had responded to a Carterlist ad from someone who needed a roommate to move in and help out with the bills. I thought it was the best decision I could have made to help start my life fresh again.

When I initially had the conversation with the lady over the phone she seemed so sweet. She told me she was an instructor at a college, and she was an American even though she had an accent, but I didn't really care about that. She asked me where I worked, and the moment I told her I worked as a Home Health Aide she said she felt reassured that since I worked in people's home's I must be trustworthy.

When I went to check out the room it felt perfect, and I moved in the next day, paying the lady in cash. The neighborhood was a bit scary, but I felt better knowing there was a school right across the street, and I could see other races like the Asian couple downstairs and the Caucasian lady upstairs.

The lady I was renting from tried her best to make me comfortable by showing me things around, she even introduced me to her daughter and her nephew that visited often. I changed the locks on the door, I was nervous to do so because I didn't want her to think I didn't trust her, but I still did it anyway. My laptop had been having problems and I hadn't had money to fix it, so she allowed me to use her computer briefly and secretly tapped her neighbor's Wi-Fi connection.

I hadn't opened my email in forever, I had 10,000 emails, almost all from advertisers. As I scrolled down, I noticed one particular email from someone I had learned to forget the hard way. The email was from Wale. I froze up at the screen. I began to read the email and it said -

The title read: I looked everywhere for your number, but I couldn't find it.

The email read:

Dear Funke,

This is Wale. I wanted to write you to say how sorry I am for how I treated you. I was scared. The feelings were all too much for me. I was scared with school, and my parents, and friends....it was too much for me and I ran.

I don't want you to feel like I never recognized that what I did was wrong. I know it was wrong. I know it hurt you very much. I suck for what I did, and I am so sorry. If there is any way I could apologize to you over the phone or in person, it would be my greatest honor.

I have a pain in my chest for how I made you feel. I am so sorry for that... so sorry....

I hope you can forgive me. I hope you do not harbor

ill will towards me. I had some of the best times of my life with you. Everything about our friendship and relationship was real. I don't want you to ever feel that it wasn't.

If it wasn't.... I wouldn't be writing you right now...almost two years later.

I am so sorry. Please find it in your heart to forgive me. I know wounds do not heal fast but at least this is my attempt at starting the healing process.

I miss your friendship, although I understand things have changed and we are both in very different places in our lives at this point.

You really helped me a lot and I just want you to know how much I am sorry.

Wale

After I read his email I started to respond with an angry sentence, then I deleted it. I started to write again with a neutral tone, then I deleted it. I realized I just wasn't ready mentally to bring him even an inch into my life. The worst part was, I couldn't even tell him, "You have kids and I gave them up for adoption."

Chapter 33

In the beginning, the lady I was living with seemed too good to be true, I even boasted about her kindness at work with my clients. But after a while, she started making smart remarks to me in the house, saying things like, "Oh wow, you cooking that African stuff that smells up the house again," or sometimes she would say, "Are you still working? I notice you only leave the house at night," not knowing I had switched to night shifts at my agency. It seemed like she monitored my every move, which was just the way my mother had acted. I started to avoid the lady by any means, and just stayed in my room when I came home, only coming out for bath times and to go to work. I mostly ate takeout food from the Chinese restaurant or the nearby corner stores.

Slowly the lady started to reveal herself, and I should have taken my cue to leave, but I foolishly turned a blind eye. She was worried about my job situation, while she herself wasn't going to work, but I didn't question her to avoid confrontation. At times she would bring in potheads, calling them her family. When I was at a very vulnerable moment, the lady and this so-called family got me comfortable with drugs. I had said no to the drugs so many times, but she pressured me to try them, promising they would soothe the pain, and stop reminding me of everything I had been through.

She told me that even though the media makes drugs look bad, the truth was that the Government wanted to make money selling them through a legal way, but we black individuals were shortening their portion for more dollars. I don't know why I believed this speech, but she convinced me when she told me that she had had abortions and heartbreaks and had used drugs to recover. She even brought out her teaching certificate to show me that she was sane enough to teach, so I should trust her.

It wasn't until I became a part of her circle that I learned she had literally robbed the government.

Stolen Sanity

The apartment had been provided by the government for her mother who had died three years ago and she just took it over. Then she made money by renting the place out to people for $500 per month when it was only costing her $200 dollars per month. When she told me this, I was way too high to analyze it or realize that I should really leave such bad company, and anyway it didn't matter, I was enjoying the good life of drugs.

The first time I had tried weed was in a brownie, and when I tried smoking it through a rolled up paper it felt different. It didn't make me go crazy or hallucinate, just made me feel like I was on cloud nine. The lady had all different kinds of people who would come through with just a phone call: the weed crew, the cocaine crew, and more. The moment I dove my head into cocaine I knew it was my last moment as a sane girl, but I thought doing it would ease my pain and help me to escape the suicidal thoughts I had been having since giving up my kids. I was a hypocrite, back in the old days I had blamed Sandra's husband for using drugs, but here i was diving in and sniffing my life away.

I lost my job because I called off work too many times. When I sniffed cocaine I went mentally blank, barely even aware of my surroundings, and I wanted more of it even though I didn't understand why. I couldn't stop myself from having more of it, I couldn't eat or sleep much, and when I wasn't high I would have unexplained anger towards people. I lost a lot of weight, the cocaine was becoming like food to me, and I got mad when I could not have it. I got disoriented in the house - I would be taking a shower and just come out of the shower and sit on the kitchen table to dry off, and then lay on the kitchen floor afterwards.

Another drug the lady had made me try was embalming fluid. She said not a lot of people knew about it, so we were "lucky to be the first generation to try it." The lady had so much passion and happiness when she talked about drugs, it was like she was giving motivational lectures.

Embalming fluid is a mixture of chemicals used to preserve dead bodies, it is a mixture of formaldehyde, methanol, and a few other things. Sometimes people brought tobacco or marijuana cigarettes that had been soaked in embalming fluid and then dried. The code words for these special weed rolls were Wet, Illy, and Fry. The embalming fluids were mostly stolen from funeral homes and passed into the street, it was a long process of insanity.

I had my very first threesome with some guys whose names I never knew and I never got a chance to clearly see how they looked either. The threesome was unwanted, but I was off the roof with the Wet messing with my mind. The only thing I knew about those men was that she had invited them in and that I felt their bodies as they touched me. I did not ever agree to two naked men taking turns to viscously and aggressively penetrate me in that horrible manner. While it was happening, I could hear the lady laughing in the background saying, "My nigga give her that pipe, fuck the bitch real good."

At the time, the Wet was working its way along to mess me up further, so all I could do was lay there without enough energy to refuse anyone. They used me like a sex doll and later, when I was a little bit saner, I began to question the lady about what had happened that night.

We argued and argued, and out of nowhere my roommate punched me in the face! I went and locked myself in my room to call the police officers. When the police officer arrived, they were asking me stupid questions and acted like I was supposed to undress and show them my private parts for inspection right there and then. They asked me to show proof I was punched, but I couldn't function properly, as I was trying so hard to hide the fact that I was still slightly high off the Wet. The police officers left the scene, not taking me seriously.

I stepped out to the grocery store for a little, bit still angry and wanting more of the cocaine or Wet but I couldn't ask my roommate for it as we were not in a good place. I came back from the grocery store only to find my belongings were outside on the floor at the main entrance. I got so angry I started to scream and shout in the hallway, hitting the walls and screaming my roommate's name.

      I was able to force open the door, and as I entered my mind took me straight to the kitchen and I grabbed a large knife. I went into her room and then checked the bathroom, but I couldn't find her, so I waited for her outside and when I saw her going back in, I ran after her and stabbed her. I didn't realize what I had done because I was still high off of the Wet. The police officers however returned and cuffed me and took me away. The newspapers the next day reported:

Saturday, July 4, 2012 @09:45pm CST

      A woman living in Bloomingdale, Illinois, who was accused of stabbing her neighbor two weeks ago, pleaded not guilty Saturday in McMor County Court. The 24-year- old Funke Adedayo is charged with aggravated battery and home invasion. Police officers at the scene claim Funke

Adedayo stabbed a neighbor three times in the shoulder, back, and side with a large kitchen knife in a dispute early Sunday.

The roommate, Anne Garyheart, 32, was treated at Sittle Regional Medical Center and later released.

The incident occurred about 2:15 a.m. in the 500 block of East Pine Avenue, said Bloomingdale Police spokesman Daniel Brown. Adedayo was held Monday in lieu of $10,000 bail on charges of aggravated battery and home invasion.

Brown said police were called to East Pine Avenue about 12:50 a.m. after Adedayo complained about being attacked.

In court Monday, a prosecutor said Adedayo claimed she also had been punched and had to change clothing because of a bloody nose. She became defensive when police asked to see the clothing, he said.

Brown said officers couldn't find any sign of injury to verify Adedayo's complaint. The prosecutor said

Adedayo threatened to have "her people" resolve the problem because police wouldn't. Brown said police officers left without any arrests but were called back about 2:15 a.m. after Anne

Garyheart was stabbed. Police Officers arrested Adedayo and found a knife believed to have been used in the attack on a kitchen counter in the apartment.

The prosecutor said Garyheart briefly had left her home and was returning when Adedayo followed her inside and stabbed her.

Chapter 34

My day in court came on July 25th. The judge decided I was guilty and deported me back to Nigeria as my school visa had expired. The officers cuffed me and shoved me in the back seat for the drive to the airport. It was a long ride and an uncomfortable one, when I complained about anything like bumping my head thanks to their speeding, they would say, "Shut the fuck up bitch, you going back to your country."

The one driving even said, "I'm tired of all you immigrants coming here and causing more crime, like fucking stay in your country." He threatened to hit me if I didn't stop speaking. He said if he did, no one would care or hear about it because I was being deported and would never to come back to the United States of America. They dropped me at a temporary facility in the airport, where I spent a night without food. It was terrible to see all the other people being deported back to their countries treated so unfairly, but since we were all criminals it didn't matter.

We all slept on the floor in a huge room with just one single toilet. There were maybe 25 of us, both men, women and children, in that room and just one toilet with no tissue. If you had to use the toilet, you had to go in front of everyone, with the whole room staring at you. Finally, one of the aircraft was able to give me a seat for my deportation process. They called my name and I was handed over to an official who rode on the plane with me all the way to Atlanta, where I had a layover, and then I was transferred to another official who rode the plane with me all the way to Nigeria. Upon reaching Nigeria I was transferred to the Nigerian Police officers who were ruthless and wicked. First off, they put me in a room and put the cuffs back on my hands. The police officer cursed at me saying, "Your father and mother sent you abroad to go and study in the white man's country, and then you disgrace Nigeria, you are a fool, if you look at me one time I will give you a dirty slap".

I rolled my eyes when he spoke to me, not so much because of what he said, but because his breath was stinking. He had horrible body odor as he stood beside me, and on his face he had a deep cultural village mark. I had never been in a situation where a police officer is supposed to take me back home, but before we could get there he made multiple stops.

First he went to grab food at the restaurant on the upper level from a girl that seemed to be getting something personal from him, as she blushed all through their talk. The next stop was at the ticket counter, where he collected money from one of the guys behind the register, the man gave him a handshake and placed the cash in his hands. The next stop was to give money to a soldier who stood at the airport entrance, they talked about a recent football match while I stood there with my cuffs on my hands. He gave my whole history to each and every one he stopped by to see, always ending my story with "foolish pikin" which means "foolish child".

When we finally got to the car, it turned out to be full with many police officers who needed a lift to the station we were heading to. Some of the police officers even sat on each other's laps in the back seat. They put me in the back of the truck, the open cargo area of the jeep. I felt like a big buffalo that had been tied up on its way to be slaughtered and cooked for dinner as I rolled and tossed in the back, bouncing at every speed bump and pot holes on the road.

Once I got to the station I was able to make a phone call to my mother. I knew by this time she would have been back in Nigeria and was settling into her kingdom as she had hoped. She was shocked and devastated to hear that I had been deported. She kept crying over the phone saying, "My life has finished oh! The child has killed me!" She repeated this over and over until the police officer grabbed the phone to tell me that his phone credit wasn't that much. She didn't even come to the police station until two days later. At that time, I was called into the office of the man in charge at the police station. As soon as

I stepped in I saw my mother sitting in front of him.

General: "This girl, you are a disgrace, so this is your mother?"

My Mother: "Oga, see my life with this shameful girl."

General: "Why would you go all the way to America and embarrass your family like this?"

My Mother: "Stupid girl, I don't even want to look at her!"

Me: "You don't even care."

My Mother: "Is it me you are talking to?"

General: "Would you shut up!? Is that how you should talk to your mother?"

My Mother: "Oga leave her, that's the bad attitude she has picked up in America."

General: "This is Nigeria, next time you try it I will stand up and slap you to the other side of this office."

My Mother: "Maybe it is even better they deported her, now she can learn how to appreciate me as her mother."

General: "I don't even know what all these children

see in this America, it's the same America that has serial killers and women having sex with bulldogs and horses, and men putting their penis' inside goats and marrying the goats."

My Mother: "Oga, America is generally good, but some people are just crazy."

General: "Me I don't want to go to a crazy country like that."

My Mother: "Anyway, like I was saying, how can you help me sir, please?"

General: "Madam why are you even helping this girl?"

My Mother: "I am a single mother, I have lost one of my daughters already. The other girl doesn't care about me anymore, and now this one has been deported. Please have mercy on me sir, I beg you in Jesus' name. Don't look at her, look at me and pity me please."

General: "Madam I understand, but she is supposed to serve her time here with a bond as instructed. I understand you were a police woman yourself, you should know we are supposed to follow protocols."

My Mother: "I know sir, and I'm not telling you how to do your job, but please, is there anything I can do? Please!"

General: "Hmm . . . OK Madam, in that case lets settle this the Naija way."

My Mother: "Which is?"

General: "Settle me and we are done here, and she is free."

My Mother: "That is no problem sir, I will take care of you. In fact, I came prepared."

General: "Now you are talking my language Madam!"

My mother dug deep into her bag, brought out two huge stacks of Nigerian currency, and put them on the table. She mentioned that it was 500,000 Naira. The moment the General saw the stack of money on the table his face lit up with a very big smile and he rubbed his beard. He stretched out his hand and grabbed the stacks of cash, counted it all com pletely like a professional. Once he was done counting the money he gave a nod and that finalized the business transaction. My mother rained every curse possible down on me on the whole way home, telling me she was ashamed of me in every possible way.

Chapter 35

I had no idea where to start in Lagos, Nigeria. My life was over, I had been gone for so long and I couldn't get a job because I never did the NYSC training required by the government. I had messed up all my opportunities and given up my children for adoption in the United States. Usually when people come back to Nigeria it was because they had finished school, had worked and saved up money to come back and start a business, but my story was one of total failure.

My mother had retired from the police force in Lagos, and had started to concentrate on being a landlord, living off the money from all her buildings and enjoying her retirement. She also had three stores in the Balogun Market, the newest of which was a clothing store selling laces, shoes and bags. My mother had asked me to accompany her to the store because she didn't want me just sitting in the house or, more likely, inviting anyone into her house that might take her expensive belongings. She had discussed handing the newest store over to me to operate as a way to help me better myself rather than sitting in my pool of shame and beating myself up on a daily basis. It would also help disguise the reason why I came back, making it look like I came back to open a store and settle down. I had thought a lot about running into friends I hadn't seen in a very long time and all of the questions they would ask me, so I started to get myself in the frame of mind of accepting that the store was mine.

      My mother was also advertising the store as mine and directing people to come to me with all their questions. The moment the doors opened floods of customers and workers from the neighboring stores came rushing in to either shop, size me up, or steal. It was a common rule at the market to never leave your phone or personal belongings just lying around because some customers would act like they were shopping but really came to steal.

When a customer came to steal, they would usually bring a friend along to act as a distracttion decoy. That friend would be responsible for asking questions and for different sizes, and while the owner was busy looking for sizes and answering questions, the first friend would be stuffing laces into a huge bag. Usually, by the time you noticed something had been stolen it would be way too late.

Many women in the market place believed in spiritual powers, they thought that if they weren't selling very much that it probably meant someone had done some witchcraft or casted a spell over their store. It was part of the daily routine to sweep, mop, and wash the front of the store before settling down for the day. The electricity system wasn't stable like the United States, in Lagos you had to have a generator on standby in case the power was taken away. The electricity was shared, what I mean by that is the Eastside might have light at 2PM, but it would go off randomly and then be given to the Westside who may have had no electricity all throughout the night. Those without a generator would have to sit in the heat and wouldn't be able to light up their stores or homes.

I interviewed sales associates to help me in the store, but it was a different process than in the United States. There wasn't a formal interview with questions like, "What are you going to bring to our brand," or "Why are you applying to this store?" The most common way of finding a sales associate in Nigeria was to ask a next door neighbor or friend who might know someone that could start work immediately.

You could specify if you wanted a male or a female associate to come work. There were two type of sales associates; the ones that came to meet you at the store every day and went back to their homes every day, and the ones who were brought from a village into the city for work, they would usually live with you and follow you into the store. The ones that lived with you would usually get paid a little bit more for doing housework in addition to working at the store - it was an around-the-clock work. I felt bad for them when their boss would call them in the middle of the night to come switch off a fan or kill a rat for them.

The person who introduced you to the sales associate would collect a fee on each one he brought in. Many families in the villages would offer their kids to come work in the city and would have the kid's salary sent back home. I requested both a male and female sales associate. I wanted a male to be handy and help me lift heavy stuff, like moving the generator from the front of the store to the back every day, and the female to help out in giving advice with all female body types.

Eventually, my mother started coming to my store more often. She left her other two stores in the hands of the sales associates and distant family members she had placed there. My mother started to get on my nerves, she started telling me how to arrange the products in the store, and requesting to see the account book of what was sold every day, and taking all the money made in the store leaving me with nothing. One time she came to collect the money and then headed out to a gathering, leaving me with so little money that I had to walk over to the neighboring store to borrow money just to get home. It was so embarrassing.

Sometimes my mother would get mad at me and scream at me in the middle of the store, the way she was acting, people in the neighborhood started to question if I truly was in charge of the store.

Some days my mother would take the keys to the store and warn me not to come close or she would embarrass me in front of everyone at the market. One day I ignored her, and she came to the store screaming at me and flinging my food and shopping bags into the dirty mud on the walk way. I watched the people stepping on my belongings as they walked by. The other market workers seemed sympathetic to my face, but behind our backs they would laugh at us. My mother's actions showed that she wanted me to give the store back to her, but she was a terrible manager. It had been two months since I had come back from the United States, and in those two months my mother had managed to go through at least five sales associates. Some left just because they were tired of her giving them hell, it made me wish that I could escape, but I was blood – it wasn't possible.

To take my mind off of stuff, I enrolled in a driving school. I also had a personal driving instructor who came on Sundays to practice with me since I was in the store Monday through Saturday. My mother gave one of her five cars to use for practice and for my personal errands and coming to the store. Whenever we argued about things at home, she would punish me by grabbing back the cars keys so I had to suffer on the dangerous public transportation system. The public bus drivers always drove extremely recklessly, so I would be praying continuously from the moment I got on until I reached my destination. The yellow buses had no compassion for life, when you reached your destination they barely came to a full stop, and you would have to jump out while they were still moving - good luck to the women who wore heels.

At that time there was a dangerous scam

going on called "One Chance." It was a fake yellow public bus filled with ritualists and thieves. The driver was part of the team, along with the conductor and two passengers. They would drive through unknown areas claiming they were taking short cuts, only to stop in dead zones, pull out guns, and steal from the passengers, leaving their dead bodies on the floor.

Chapter 36

    I knew my mother had turned into a completely cold person the day I tried to help my driving instructor carry a gallon of water. We had been driving back and forth from my house to his, and on the very last run he asked if he could put a gallon of water in the car so that when we drove past his house he could drop it off instead of carrying it there on his head. I said yes and put the gallon in my trunk, as I started to reverse I heard my mum screaming our names.

    She called me on the phone shouting, "Are you crazy? Why is he using that expensive car to carry his cheap gallon of water? Tell him to take that gallon of water out of the car now!" I hung up the phone and continued reversing, but this time she called his phone and told him directly. We had to park the car back in its spot and hand over the keys to her as he took his gallon of water out to carry on his head. Even though this man was getting paid to come help me, I thought it was no big deal to also help him in a little way, but my mother thought otherwise. The man never returned after that, and thanks to my mum that was the end of my driving lessons. She had succeeded in taking the store back and now she had taken the car back as well.

    The next time we argued she told me to move out of her house, and I did just that - leaving the keys with my cousin who was in the house with us. The man guarding the entrance gate asked me nervously, "I'm sorry madam, please don't fire me for this question, but why is your mother so tough on you like this? She fights you like her enemy!"

    I just smiled and told him it was the story of my life. I had nowhere to go, so I told the salon owner next door my situation. She told me to hang around until nighttime and that when she closed up the store she would let me sleep over at her place until I figured out where to go next. It turned out we couldn't make it to her house that evening because there was some sort of memorial remembrance for an area boy who had just died going on in the street.

The mourners were breaking bottles in the road, throwing fire flames and literally just scaring people off the streets. We both slept that night in her salon, closing ourselves in and lighting candles throughout. The salon owner advised me, despite what I had told her, to go back and show forgiveness to my mother and try to reconcile. She said it was just the Godly thing to do to forgive people that hurt us.

It was interesting that she said that, because when daylight came and we opened the doors to the salon, the first thing we saw were police officers standing out front with my mother. The officers cuffed the owner of the salon, saying she was harboring a criminal. My mother said she wanted to deal with me herself, so they escorted me back into her house. I don't know why she would tell me to move out then come and force me to move back in, but these back and forth movements were typical of her.

I was drained and needed a distraction, so I

started going to parties I had heard about on the radio or through fliers I saw at the stores. I attended a lot of parties since there wasn't much else to do, and through those parties I started getting back into drugs. The parties had huge containers of drugs, I guess the shipping agents must have been bribed to bring it in. One night I went to a closed private party on an island, I got in through a random high-ranking man who claimed me as his girl at the door. I just went with the flow and got in successfully.

      There were local celebrities present at this party purchasing drugs to take to back to their homes. I could have stopped myself from getting into this craziness once again, but I felt the urge. I had missed it. I was depressed, I was suicidal, and so I dug in and sniffed my life away. At one point I found myself spread on a table as the guy that brought me in fingered me continuously. I didn't refuse him, I let him do it to me because I wasn't sane anymore, I was so high that I lost my pride and became loose.

      The next morning i found myself braless with my

breasts hanging out in all their glory. I don't even have the slightest idea of what happened that night. I was on the floor of an unconstructed site of an uncompleted building, only God knows how I traveled from the party to the place I woke up. I grabbed a very tiny piece of clothing, that seemed to have been used as a head wrap, to cover my breasts and used the last money I had on me to take a taxi home.

      I finally got home around 1PM. The house boy was in the hallway, sitting on the floor just looking worried and lost. He had not eaten he said, and my mother had been out since morning, I gave him some food from the kitchen since it was a taboo for the house boy to put his hand in the pot of stew that the boss had cooked.

      While he was eating I was just sitting aimlessly in the living room. There was no electricity and there was nothing to do, I couldn't put on the generator as there was no petrol. After a few hours, after I had taken a quick nap out of boredom, I reached over to look at the documents my mother had left on the table near her room. The papers were receipts for land close to the Ajah area that she had just sold to someone for about 7.9 million Naira. There were also receipts she had written for tenants who had paid their rent recently. I got so angry looking at these documents - here I was suffering, she had taken back the store she gave me, along with the money I made at the store, and the whole time she had all this money flowing into her account yet she was still fighting me over hundreds.

      I was so angry I started pacing back and forth. I entered my room and dipped my head into the cocaine I had stolen from the party, stashed in a nylon. As I kept waiting for my mum to return, I rolled up some weed as well from my little kit. I grew even angrier remembering all the money she had, running my hands through my hair wondering how all of a sudden money was flowing in from all of these lands she had which I wasn't even sure how she got in the first place. Around evening I sent the houseboy to buy something for himself, but he refused to take the money telling me my mother had said if he ever took money from me she would break his head. I told him to go buy whatever he wanted, and I wouldn't tell her anything, but that he should go quickly before she came back home.

Chapter 37

Just a few minutes after he left, I heard her pressing the horn outside. Usually when she honks her car at the gate she expects the houseboy to come and open it, but he wasn't around. I waited for her in the living room, not moving an inch from where I sat. Finally, she walked into the house calling the houseboy's name. She moved the curtains to the side and saw me sitting in her usual spot in the living room.

Mother: "Ah ah, so you are around, and you heard me pressing the car horn outside and calling the house boy's name?"

I didn't respond.

Mother: "I'm talking to you, are you deaf?"

Me: "How much did you make today?"

Mother: "Excuse me?"

Me: "I said how much did you make today?"

Mother: "What kind of foolish question is that?"

Me: "It's the kind of question a frustrated daughter would ask a selfish mother who doesn't care."

Mother: "Funke! Why are you so angry? I've never seen you look at me in this manner. Are you okay?"

Me: "No, I am not okay, I am disgusted that you can have millions in your account and can't even give me a common 100,000 to start my life again, or at least use it to find my way to a better condition."

Mother: "Look, I am tired, I am a single mother, I am the mother, I am the father, I am everything. Do you think it is easy?"

Me: "You have never asked me what I really wanted to do, every time I tried to talk to you, even about the real estate job, you told me to get out of your sight, the next time I asked, you said we will talk later."

Mother: "So because I cannot give you the job you want and the money, you want to now beat me up Abi?"

Me: "You are very selfish! You are very wicked!"

Mother: "Me? Your mother?"

Me: "Yes, you!"

Mother: "God will punish you, you foolish child."

Me: "God will do the same for you because you are wicked!"

Mother: "Continue to abuse me, you have no respect for me whatsoever, I would have aborted you if I knew you would be a devil!"

Me: "Well if I am the devil, then I am definitely your reflection."

Mother: "I see you have gone mad, you are useless as a woman and as a human being. No job at your age, your mates have graduated and married the men of their dreams. They are preparing to have children and bless their parents with gifts, but all you accomplished is having bastard children from the devil you slept with. You are a prostitute, used product, your life is worthless at this point."

Me: "OHHHH! So you want to act holier than thou when you had three abortions before Sandra, Funmi and I? You have failed as a mother, building hatred between your children. All you are passionate about is money, that's why you are greedy and love your so-called golden daughter Sandra. Where is Sandra now? When last did your precious daughter call you? You made me give up my children because you could not bear to see me happy despite my wedlock situation."

Mother: "Shut UP!! Leave my house now!!! You will never return to this house and never cross my path ever again. I disown you!"

Me: "Oh please, I disown you as a mother. Who wants a mother that silences the mouth of a child that constantly tells you that she was raped? You fucking bitch, you let your brother, that fool I call Uncle, rape me when I was little. I will tell everyone what is going on in this foolish family, including you using Funmi for money rituals."

Mother: "Me? Use my own daughter for money rituals?"

She slapped me across the face so hard that I immediately dished back a hard slap across her face in response. She grabbed me by the neck and pushed me straight into the tall mirror standing at the back wall, which immediately shattered. The crash caused my late sister Funmi's picture to fall down off the wall. I grabbed her face and was pressing my fingers into her eyes, she started to grip my neck tighter saying, "I will kill you before you kill me!"

I heard this and got even more defensive, by this time I don't truly think the sane part of me was present anymore. It felt like my blood was boiling and this person on top of me was no longer my mother, she had turned into an enemy before my eyes. I kept thinking I had to do something to win this battle, the fact that she struck me after I revealed something I had never talked about to anyone pushed me into a very angry and uncontrollable place.

I started to strike her on her face, and she released her hand from my neck and started striking me back. I pulled her hair, and she tightened her fist and started punching me directly in the face. I started to lose control, she was heavy on top of me, and I struggled to push her off. She rose up from me screaming, "I will kill you today foolish child, just like her father!" She ran toward her room looking for something and at that moment I spotted the sledgehammer. Mum ran back in and she threw a chair at me, as I felt it hit my head, I went for her and struck her with the hammer. I don't know what was controlling me, all I knew was that I struck her, and she fell.

   The second time I struck her with the sledgehammer she pleaded for me to stop. I have never heard her be less than controlling, so when she begged me it only angered me more, and I kept on pounding the sledgehammer right into her face until it damaged her skull and left her unrecognizable. I had no compassion, I felt at that moment that I had ended all my problems, I felt like I had finally punished her for what she put me through all my life. I stood up - all my clothes were bloody, my hands were bloody, and the rug was filled with blood. I didn't think of myself as a murderer, I just felt like I had solved my problem.

    I washed my hands clean, changed my outfit, and immediately grabbed more cocaine to sniff my life away. I went into her purse and grabbed the keys, her phone, and all the cash. That night I put the house boy up in a hotel, I checked in, paid for the hotel in my name, and left him there to sleep. I returned to my mother's house and locked the door with her dead body inside. Then I walked down the block to meet my regular weed suppliers. The money I had taken from her bag should have been used to flee the scene like I had seen in the movies, but because I wasn't totally sane at the time, so I just used it to get me more weed and some drinks and to chill with the guys in their house.

    It wasn't until two days later that I called Sandra from my mother's phone. As soon as she picked up and said "Hello," I froze. She said "Hello," again, and finally I said, "It's me, Funke." Sandra laughed and replied, "What do you want?" I said, "I have killed your mother," and hung up.

Biodun Abudu

Tinent Newspaper

Daughter Kills Mother

September 21, 2013

"Yes, I am the murderer, I am not just a suspect, I will tell you the truth, I killed my mum because she is a witch," said Funke Adedayo, who is in police custody for allegedly killing her 62-year-old mother.

There was nothing to suggest remorse.

She looked calm and seemed in full control of her senses.

Not even the suggestion that she may be of unsound mind carried weight when, in a clear voice, Adedayo Funke brazenly stated: "I am not a suspect. I am a murderer." When she spoke those words at the Police Command Headquarters yesterday, someone said, "She has confessed. The police have had their job made much easier." State Police spokesman, Mr.

Frederick Meme said the police would need the assistance of a psychiatrist to know the true state of Adedayo's mind, however preliminary investigations revealed that the suspect might have been under the influence of hard drugs when she committed the crime.

The suspect was arrested by the Akota Divisional Headquarters Area D on September 16, after a report reached the police that she had killed her mother at their private home.

Adedayo Funke is a graduate of Accountancy from the Chicago State University in the United States of America. She confessed to being a cocaine addict from the age of nine and was sexually abused by her uncle at the age of three.

"I have two children in the United States of America, but I gave them up for adoption.

When I came back to Nigeria, I started working for my mum. But she was not paying me well. I got angry because she is very rich. I saw her writing checks for millions of dollars to other people, but any time I asked her for money she would not give me any."

Adedayo said she had previously been jailed in Chicago, IL USA for attempted murder. "I was living in the US and one of my neighbors had an issue with me over the laundry machine. After that issue, I went to jail and I decided to come back to Nigeria."

Miss Adedayo blamed her mother for her drug addiction. "My mum introduced me to cocaine at the age of nine, and since then I have been an addict. After taking crack cocaine one day, I had a flashback to my uncle raping me when I was 3 years old and all the things I had gone through. I began to cry, and I asked our house help, Sesan, if anybody had ever touched him in a way he does not like. Sesan told me that my mum did and that my mum had also given him cocaine.

"I wondered why my mum would have sex with Sesan and it made me mad, I remembered we used to be poor and suddenly we had become rich because my mum used my sister Funmi for money rituals."

The suspect said she used a sledge hammer to kill her mother.

"My mum tried to take the hammer from me and we started fighting. I overpowered her and hit her with the hammer on the head, she just slumped and died," she said.

When the suspect saw that her mother had died, she said she told the house help to pour acid on the body.

Police spokesperson Fredrick Meme confirmed the incident.

Mr. Meme said, "After committing the crime on September 16, the suspect took the house help and they went to lodge in a hotel. She put a call to her sister in the US telling her that she had killed their mother."

"The case was reported to the police two days later and they went to the house and saw the lifeless body of the victim lying in a pool of blood."

"From her confession, it was a combination of many factors. She needs a psychiatrist and we need to decide if she committed the crime in her lucid period or as a result of the drugs she has been taking."

By Patrick Gambo

Comment 1

I will advise all the readers; what you don't know, you don't judge. This is a family I know well. I don't think the mother was wrong for sending her daughter abroad to study. It's just that the girl mingled with the wrong set of people. My prayer for every parent is that our children's destiny should not be manipulated. As far as I am concerned, this case is beyond physical, there is more to this case than what people are saying. She was a girl that was in a choir in a reputable church in Chicago when she first got to America, very loyal and respectful. Oh my God, this is sad. May the mother's soul rest in peace.

Comment 2

I think it's quite unfortunate that this happened. I don't have the habit of judging people no matter what they've done, because I believe there are things we do that no one knows about. I am in no way trying to commend what she has done, but at the same time not condemning her. We are all humans with blood running through our veins. Some of us have killed in one way or the other, through abortion and other sorts. We just need to know how to forgive and learn what there is to learn from any situation and move forward. I feel sorry for her, and I pray she gets the help she needs. I pray God forgives her.

Comment 3
Nigerians, where is our sense of empathy?! The family deserves our sympathy and prayers, and not these judgmental comments. Some of us are plain unknowledgeable, or should I just say ignorant, and talk outside of the box at times.

Comment 4

These Yoruba people again! They are our problem in this country. I think this lady had a major issue with her mother over the house boy who is probably the lady's lover as well.

Comment 5
It's such a shame. I went to secondary school with her. She had thick thighs back then. It was quite lovely seeing her going to the dinner hall 'cause her ass jiggled a lot.

Comment 6
This is sad. I actually know her, though my memory of her is vague. My family and I lived in their house for some years. Her mom is a policewoman and her grandmother was a suspected witch as well. Thank God my family moved out of that house.

Comment 7
Her mother was a police woman, does that ring a bell? She may have been part of those that con-

tributed to the looting of our countries funds and sent their children abroad, only for them to become a nuisance which eventually kills them. This is a lesson for our leaders who are presently looting our resources and sending their children abroad while sabotaging the education of this country and other things. I hope the curse issued on them each day by hurting people will not cause their children to come home one day and kill them!

Chapter 38

There was a combination of sympathetic, ignorant, and random comments from people that both somewhat knew me, and from those who didn't know me at all, that filled all the newspapers that published the murder story that week. The police force had great fun making a mockery of me, they made several videos of me during this time when I was not okay just speaking without thinking. They made fun of my American accent during my court cases and in the prison cells, I became quite popular within the prison because of my accent. I was made to sit down with psychiatrists who had no idea of what I had been through. They only knew of the recent event that had brought me to their facility. I was trying to bring myself back to a being normal while waiting for them to decide my faith.

I was told my high school friend Oyinkan wouldn't visit me because it would be bad for her image, she had become a popular Nigerian actress, and was too good to grace me with her presence. I couldn't blame her as we had fallen off with our communication since I left for the United States. My family members stayed clear of me at first, until finally one or two came to see me. They told me that Sandra had conducted a funeral service for our mother. I was also told that she cancelled me out of our mother's will because of what I had done. So many people called me names or said things to me like they knew my story or what I had been carrying before this event. With a pen and paper that I took from the prison guard I wrote an open note to kill my boredom, to give myself a therapeutic moment in the cell.

Call me the queen of sorrow, just when I think I am saved from pain, suddenly disaster blesses my feet. I have lost the use of my heart and yet I am still alive, for what reason I'm not sure yet. The same song swirls through my bloodstream, its title, "Is it my time yet?" I look around the jail cell to end myself faster rather than be hung to die for what I have done or to be shot at a firing squad or possibly stoned to death.

A counsellor once looked me in my eyes and tried to tell me what pain was. I remember grabbing the wheels, grabbing the mic, and turning the tables and letting her know she knew nothing at all about pain. She only seemed to get paid to listen to stories and repeat the words, "I understand," without a clue as to what pain really is. With no idea of what it is to say suicidal prayers every night because you are just about done.

Nothing will change or wipe away your past, especially if there are scars to remind you. On the outside everything looks perfect, but if I entered your parish and I dropped my robe you would see my body filled with scars, blood dripping down my skin, signatures of molestation, dedicated rapists marks, and a certain glow on my skin I always called family neglect.

We were born into sin, and we are all sinners, constantly sinning, yet I am put to the forefront of sin, *and I alone to bear the consequences. That's the atmosphere and the world I live in. A world where the pastor has to read my Wikipedia profile full of sins before he can decide if I am worth helping so as not to put shame upon his name and his parish. The reputation of a parish or a family name is worth more than saving a soul these days.*

The prison had church members come and preach to us, I prayed majorly for forgiveness of what I had done. I looked to the moon every night thinking of my past, and I looked to the sun thinking of my future, wondering if I would ever have one again outside these walls. Time will only tell, as I await my sentence, either way I just wish the world would let me see my children once again before I give my last breath within these prison walls. I wake up every day not knowing my fate; if I will be released from prison, if I will stay a certain amount of years, or if I will be sentenced to death.

Chapter 39

There as a time during my stay in jail about a year after that I got a very random visit from my late sister's ex. He sat down and told me he had seen me on the news channel that aired different stories from the prison cell and my story was also part of the segment. He had mentioned that on so many accounts he had wanted to visit me but my family which were my aunties, my uncles, my cousins and more had told him not to visit at all. Through him I was able to find out that most of my aunties had fled the country and had moved out of the compound where my mother had died out of fear, that I may hire some killers to come after them.

The first time he visited he told me he didn't have much time as his wife didn't know he was visiting or anyone for that matter. He did leave the current numbers of my cousins and aunts for me to call during break time in the prison cells. One of my aunties hung up the phone as she heard my voice. My cousin disappeared as I asked her for money to buy toiletries in the prison cell. In the prison we really didn't have the luxury to use toilet paper after using the bathroom, or even any sanitary pads. In place of the toilet paper we used water to clean up and the water was very dirty. In place of the sanitary pads I would just fold up paper I ripped off from a note pad to put in my panties as my sanitary pad, if I was lucky enough I could use something softer like a handkerchief that the prison guard might have left on the chair beside my cell after he had exhausted it to clean his sweat. My sister's ex eventually provided me with the provisions I needed while I was in the prison cell. He came every three months when he could, he had just had triplets, so it was a busy and tough time for him as well. My sentencing was unclear, and they had wanted to keep me as they are unsure of what to do as I was highly influenced when I committed the murder. I never really felt comfortable or bold enough to tell anyone about my rape, to be able to reveal them or tell anyone would feel like ripping layers of my skin to tell the painful story.

Eventually my late sister's ex asked me as he had read somewhere in the newspaper when I mentioned my uncle had raped me when I was younger. He stuttered before the question eventually dropped, he must have been scared to ask as he didn't know what my reaction to be.

Late sister's ex - Funke I hate to ask this question, but the newspaper said you mentioned being raped. Umm does anyone in the family know this?

Me - umm hmm

Late sister's ex - its fine if you don't want to discuss it right now or at all

Me - no one really knows except my mother

Late sister's ex - what did she say or do about this?

Stolen Sanity

Me - hmm

Late sister's ex - you can tell me anything I promise it won't leave past this room

Me - it's not even that, just the thought of how she shut me up for years to not speak on it

Late sister's ex - oh wow

Me - she did nothing but tell me to shut up, she even beat me up for bringing it up at school to my teachers

Late sister's ex - Are you serious?!!!

Me - yes, she hated when I brought it up, I learned how to keep shut and just keep the horrible flashes in my head from a young age, I'm used to it.

Late sister's ex - I'm so sorry to hear this, I didn't know you were going through this

Me - Its fine I have found ways to keep it locked away or found ways to forget about the pain for as much as I could keep it away.

Late sister's ex - you have to be able to speak to someone to fully let it go but which of your uncles did this to you? please tell me!

Me - I don't think it's even important anymore, it's been years

Late sister's ex - it been years, but someone can still face him on your behalf, God forbid what if he is doing this to other young girls?

Me - It doesn't even matter, he is not even around in Nigeria

Late sister's ex - but all your uncles are out the country please tell me which one in particular

Me - Uncle Tobi

Late sister's ex - what !!!!! are you serious? wow

Me - yes that devil

Late sister's ex - I can't even believe this, I mean I'm shocked

Me - yes, he raped me. whenever I went to visit him and his wife, especially when his wife went out. He would be sticking a broom stick in my private part and slap me if I asked too many questions. Eventually he stopped using broom sticks then he started using his hands and then he raped me. It was painful, and my mother didn't care. At times I felt as if I was a trade by barter deal my mother had made with him because not for once did she even stand up for me or have interest in listening to what happened. She has seen him on my many occasions after that and he is even the one that gave her land five years ago that she sold recently.

Late sister's ex - wow

Me - my mother still let him come pick me up from school even after I told her he raped me. I can't count the amount of times he would randomly park the car to try to force his way up into my school skirt. Sometimes she would drop me off at his place when she needed to travel. Sleeping in the house of the man that raped me wasn't the ideal childhood I would have chosen. All I could do was lock the room door behind me or find a way to sleep beside his wife at that moment, so he can't reach me. Eventually I ran to my other cousin's house to avoid seeing him.

Late sister's ex - I believe what he did is catching up with him right now

Me - what do u mean?

Late sister's ex - you don't know what happened to him? or where he is?

Me - Since he left to South Africa and Germany I haven't heard anything about him and that was years ago when I left to go to the USA

Late sister's ex - Well the last time I saw him he told me he came back home to settle down. However, your sister Funmi told me he was deported as he got into a mess with a lady that claimed he assaulted her. Wow come to think of it, he must have tried to rape the lady also.

Me - maybe not tried he probably did, I didn't know he was back all this while I was here.

Late sister's ex - As we speak he is not even himself anymore

Me - not himself? What happened to him

Late Sister ex - just sad things that happened to him

Me - is he close to dying? I would love to watch him die slowly

Late sister's ex - well he has been through a lot for the past few years

Me - oh he has? I never heard of a rapist going through a lot and people feeling sorry for him

Late sister's ex - well let me just say this. He had twins and they were both holding each other crossing the road when a car ran them over, I guess the wife couldn't bare the pain, so she left him alone. He's been depressed and not himself and recently he had a stroke. Seeing him poop, pee on himself is just not a good sight to see. He lost all his lands and businesses. Everything came crashing down all through last year which caused the stroke. It's a very sad story. He must have been cursed by someone

Me - I don't care about all that in fact I hope he dies soon. I only feel sorry for his wife and kids that had to be associated with a rapist. He is now bearing the pain he caused me and maybe other girls, the curses have now caught up with him. He is going to die soon.

Late sister's ex - hmmm well anyway I'm glad you could share this story with me, it's good to talk to someone about it. He is probably paying for his sins and God will handle it from there.

Me - yea I guess so.

After that moment I felt slightly relieved to be able to speak to someone who won't slap me across my face when I tell my rape story, it was nice to receive a hug and be told I have support and I could continue to talk about what's bothering me and be given resources to be able to get through the memories that still last in my head. After that moment he advised me to talk further to the therapists that come to check on me and I did. She shared her own story as well, she told me things to do to overcome the fears, the trauma and more. Till that very moment not even one of my family members even reached out to speak to me.

I'm very positive my dad must have heard what happened to me or my mum. No one was able to reach him directly and he never reached out to me to see me after all these years he had abandoned me and funmi. Even when Funmi died he never reached out to me to see how I was coping. My mother must have really done something to him for him to finally decide he was done with us. My family had abandoned me and have avoided my calls because of the sin I have committed.

At night I pray for the Lord's forgiveness upon my soul for what I have done. I also prayed for my family that the Lord would melt their heart to reach out to me while I am in prison. The prison started to let us engage in activities outside of our cells. I truly believe what influenced this was the visit of the Government's wife recently to the prison cells to see how things are operated. They all of a sudden had some of us get our hair done, attend church service within the prison yard of course, use the computers and more.

    However, one thing that brought a bright light to my darkness when I was able to connect to the company that did the adoption for my kids. I was able to do this during the times they allowed us to use the computers. When I connected to the adoption company I was not able to speak to my kids but I was able to get or see pictures of how they looked. I got pictures of them celebrating their birthdays, Christmas, Thanksgiving, Halloween and more. They look so happy, I'm not sure if they knew about me and if they knew about me I'm not sure if they knew where I was or if they viewed me as a bad person. I fear that if I had the opportunity to reach out to them directly they may not receive me well at all. I think that would hurt me the most amongst all I have been through. Seeing my kids reject me or shutting the door on me or saying "no you're not my mother" or "I hate you, go away." Seeing their pictures kept me happy, after I pleaded with the officials in the prison yard I was able to put their pictures beside my bed. Waking up and seeing them on the wall gave me hope for a fresh start, that is if the judge decides to set me free. For now, I still await my sentence in the prison cell as the court or judge hadn't quite decided yet. I leave it all in the hands of the Lord for he alone can give me the ultimate forgiveness for my sins knowingly and unknowingly.

Chapter 40

In historic times, family love was a very strong kind of love, it was believed to be one of the strongest bonds. Children would apologize for their mistakes, and the parents would forgive them despite what had been committed. Family love back then meant regular dinners which included all family members. The dinner was prepared by the mother, and all the family members were home right before dinner whether they were coming from school or work or wherever.

The dinner gathering was a way to keep the whole family updated on each other's lives. The husband might announce his new promotion, the kids might talk about a tough day at school. This is where the idea of family advice derived from, and kids never really had to go outside their homes for advice. A chapter I read from a book I picked up at the library hit the nail on the head when it mentioned that now sib-

-lings take each other for granted. Today's family love is not as strong.

The kids may develop a hatred towards one another in cases where their fathers are different, especially if the step dad or mum is abusive towards them. The family of today eats outside at a fast food restaurant, rather than having a dinner at home with the family. The mothers and fathers don't even know what's going on with their kids on a daily basis. The kids develop a wall and aren't comfortable sharing anything with their parents, in fact they consider that to be "awkward," or "weird," or "uncool." Once in a while we may have family gatherings when everyone's schedule can accommodate it, but we rarely even send emails or letters - we mostly text to keep in touch with family.

Young children may be hesitant to tell their parents what they experienced at a field trip, at school, or while visiting an uncle or aunt because the parents seem too busy to listen. These parents sometimes instill fear in their children and consider having a conversation with them about anything as disrespectful. How did we move into an era where parents sit on high respectable chairs, and can't even lower their heads to listen to the cries of their own children?

When abuse and rape and even worse things are kept hidden within a child, it creates individuals who live in the society with no value on family. When there is family neglect, there is no family value and it is a shame to hear parents say, "Why don't you open up or tell me anything?" It is the parent's responsibility to create a comfortable space for their kids to open up to them at a young age so it won't become an issue when they are grown. Over the years parents became way too firm and have driven away the comfort level in children to approach their parents about a problem.

When abuse and rape and worse things are hidden within those little boys and girls, it can create more pedophiles for our society. Pedophiles are occasionally a reflection of another pedophile who touched them when they were young. They may have wanted to tell someone about how they had been wrongfully touched, but there was no one around and the parents wouldn't dare to stoop so low as to engage in a conversation with their child.

Most parents know their stubborn kids well enough and they are well aware of the havoc they can create, but it is never OK to take the side of a stranger or your elder brother when your own child is crying at your knees telling you he or she has been wrongfully touched. I have a graphic video playing repeatedly in my mind about what happened between me and my uncle. I begin to tear up when I think of all the gruesome things he did to me when I was only three years old. I was just his plaything, and I didn't have a voice. I was told to lay down with my legs spread apart, and I did just as my big favorite uncle instructed me to. I would ask why, and he would tell me he was making sure I wasn't falling sick and I would grow up big and strong and healthy.

I thought maybe because he was a doctor this was true, so I didn't really fight it, but sadly the only thing that grew big and strong was his manhood whenever he lifted up my skirt. He punished me whenever I refused to play as his patient. He would slap me, throw me on his bed, and lift up my skirt. Then he would put a broom stick through my private parts and break it inside. On other days he would dip the broomstick in hot peppers and insert it in my private parts, I got a very uncomfortable burn which I didn't know how to explain to those around me. I would try and tell my mum, but she would cut me off by complaining about how I had soiled my clothes with oil, or smacking me with her slippers. I was scared that if I told her she might beat me with the cable wires. Other times, when I heard her calling me a bastard, or saying, "I should have aborted you, foolish child, and stupid like her father," I lost my courage to tell her about my sexual abuse.

    Sometimes our single mothers see in us our fathers who must have broken their hearts. It may be the reason why they treat their kids so harshly, they are too preoccupied with the pain and have no friends to share it with, so they just take it out on the kids. In my country for example, most women think that other women envy them, so they would never share anything with anyone, not even their sisters or brothers. It was always a competition, so they would rather keep things bottled up. It somehow trickled down to their kids who they compare to other women's kids saying, "Well John bought his mother a car last night, when are you going to buy me a car? You are selfish, just like that fool that calls himself your father."

Chapter 41

I once read a post online which read *"It just makes me so sad when you're watching a beautiful lady or handsome fellow talk about their passion. They light up and start bubbling over with words, and then all of a sudden they stop themselves and say, "Sorry, I know this is boring," or "Sorry, I just got excited." You realize that somewhere in their life someone they respected told them, "Shut up, nobody cares," and ever since then they can't talk about their favorite things without apologizing every five seconds. Even when they are venting about a personal problem to a therapist, they still stop to apologize during the conversation. This is one of the things that is instilled into the minds of the young ones of today and that they grow up with."*

So many of us have stories to tell, and the recovery begins when we let it out in a support group. The pain builds up when there isn't a single soul to tell, because everyone is just too busy to take a second to even look your way. Pain knows no age and knows no time. Part of me was missing and nobody would listen. I was forced to believe that Hell is a place called home. Human beings do what they do best, "judge" and point fingers and accuse, but everyone forgets when I needed someone to just listen to my story.

I've been known to make pain look good, to keep my thoughts to myself so no one ever questioned what was behind my smile. Eventually it happened - the tragedy and pain overflowing my emotions beyond ordinary levels. My walls were broken down, I saw myself heading into the dark shadows, by the time I stepped back out into the light it was too late and I didn't recognize myself anymore.

My culture held me by the throat and told me to accept it as normal like the lashes from a horse whip. My religion told me to get on my knees and pray as blood flowed down my hairline to the floor. Family neglect is the reason I slept in my pool of blood. In my pool of blood and tears I kicked back with my legs crossed, smoking away my depression. Take a walk through my journey and understand my actions, my choice of words. Summer days were for me to cater to my aching soul, winter days were for me to roam in circles, wondering if someone would lead me to sanity.

The wicked tradition, the dark secrets, the anger from deep within, my lost soul, confused state of mind, war with my own sanity, suicidal notes, and the fear of speaking out is what created who I have become . . . a *reflection of the devil.*

ACKNOWLEDGMENTS

I first of all want to thank the beautiful soul who found comfort and courage to share her story with me for the world to read and learn from.

I want to thank Eden Butler, Carol Tietsworth, Thabiso Mohohlo and Jodiann Matthews for their inputs, time and edits for this novel.

I also want to thank Henry Jimenez for bringing my art work and vision to reality for the book cover. I am trully grateful for your time and talent.

ABOUT THE AUTHOR

Biodun Abudu was born in Rhode Island, but comes from a Nigerian background. He wrote his first title "Tales of My Skin" also based on a true life story in 2011 with a revised edition in 2015. When he is not writing, he works as an Artist. In 2011, he graduated with an A.S. degree in Fashion Design, and a B.A. in Merchandising Management with an emphasis on Fashion Merchandising. He currently resides in New York City.

WWW.BIODUNABUDU.COM
INFO@BIODUNABUDU.COM

Biodun Abudu

www.ingramcontent.com/pod-product-compliance
Lightning Source LLC
Chambersburg PA
CBHW071300110426
42743CB00042B/1124